Institute of Leadership
& Management

super series

Planning Change in the Workplace

FIFTH EDITION

Published for the
Institute of Leadership & Management

ELSEVIER

AMSTERDAM • BOSTON • HEIDELBERG • LONDON • NEW YORK • OXFORD
PARIS • SAN DIEGO • SAN FRANCISCO • SINGAPORE • SYDNEY • TOKYO
Pergamon Flexible Learning is an imprint of Elsevier

Pergamon
Flexible
Learning

Pergamon Flexible Learning is an imprint of Elsevier
Linacre House, Jordan Hill, Oxford OX2 8DP, UK
30 Corporate Drive, Suite 400, Burlington, MA 01803, USA

First edition 1986
Second edition 1991
Third edition 1997
Fourth edition 2003
Fifth edition 2007

Editor: David Pardey

Based on material in previous editions of this work

British Library Cataloguing in Publication Data
A catalogue record for this book is available from the British Library

Library of Congress Cataloguing in Publication Data
A catalogue record for this book is available from the Library of Congress

ISBN 978-0-08-046444-2

For information on all Pergamon Flexible Learning publications
visit our website at http://books.elsevier.com

Institute of Leadership & Management
Registered Office
1 Giltspur Street
London
EC1A 9DD
Telephone: 020 7294 2470
www.i-l-m.com
ILM is part of the City & Guilds Group

Typeset by Charon Tec Ltd (A Macmillan Company), Chennai, India
www.charontec.com
Printed and bound in Great Britain

07 08 09 10 11   10 9 8 7 6 5 4 3 2 1

Contents

Contents

Series preface

Whether you are a tutor/trainer or studying management development to further your career, Super Series provides an exciting and flexible resource to help you to achieve your goals. The fifth edition is completely new and up-to-date, and has been structured to perfectly match the Institute of Leadership & Management (ILM)'s new unit-based qualifications for first line managers. It also harmonizes with the 2004 national occupational standards in management and leadership, providing an invaluable resource for S/NVQs at Level 3 in Management.

Super Series is equally valuable for anyone tutoring or studying any management programmes at this level, whether leading to a qualification or not. Individual workbooks also support short programmes, which may be recognized by ILM as Endorsed or Development Awards, or provide the ideal way to undertake CPD activities.

For learners, coping with all the pressures of today's world, Super Series offers you the flexibility to study at your own pace to fit around your professional and other commitments. You don't need a PC or to attend classes at a specific time – choose when and where to study to suit yourself! And you will always have the complete workbook as a quick reference just when you need it.

For tutors/trainers, Super Series provides an invaluable guide to what needs to be covered, and in what depth. It also allows learners who miss occasional sessions to 'catch up' by dipping into the series.

Super Series provides unrivalled support for all those involved in first line management and supervision.

Unit specification

Title:	Planning change in the workplace		Unit Ref:	M3.03
Level:	3			
Credit value:	2			

Learning outcomes *The learner* will	Assessment criteria *The learner* can *(in an organization with which the learner is familiar)*	
1. Understand the forces for change in an organization	1.1	Identify the forces that may require your organization to change by conducting a simple PESTLE and/or SWOT analysis
2. Understand planning for change in an organization	2.1	Give an example of change required in the workplace reflecting the SWOT and/or PESTLE analyses
	2.2	Use a tool for planning change with the context of the example given
	2.3	Identify relevant human and financial factors in the consideration of change within the context of the example given
	2.4	Explain how people can be communicated with and involved to facilitate effective change
3. Understand continuous improvement in an organization	3.1	Explain the importance of quality awareness and the need to continuously improve the organization
	3.2	Identify the organization's quality standards
	3.3	Use a continuous improvement tool or technique relevant to the workplace
	3.4	Explain ways of involving the team in quality and continuous improvement
	3.5	Discuss ways to evaluate continuous improvement activities

Workbook introduction

1 ILM Super Series study links

This workbook addresses the issues of *Planning Change in the Workplace*. Should you wish to extend your study to other Super Series workbooks covering related or different subject areas, you will find a comprehensive list at the back of this book.

2 Links to ILM qualifications

This workbook relates to the learning outcomes of Unit M3.03 Planning change in the workplace from the ILM Level 3 Award, Certificate and Diploma in First Line Management.

3 Links to S/NVQs in management

This workbook relates to the following Unit of the Management Standards which are used in S/NVQs in Management, as well as a range of other S/NVQs:

C5. Plan change

4 Workbook objectives

'Nothing is permanent but change'.

This thought was expressed by Heraclitus, a Greek philosopher living around 500 BC. At the present time in our history, when the rate of change seems to be increasing, the truth behind the above statement is self-evident, particularly when applied to the world of work.

The days when employees did the same job, in the same way, for most of their working lives are long since gone. The working environment has seen many dramatic and far-reaching changes over the last 40 years or so, and it is difficult to imagine that 'the good old days' (if ever they existed!) will return.

Change is not a single hurdle: a problem to be got out of the way before you get back to normal. Change goes on all the time. No organization and no team can afford to stand still: there's no room left for complacency.

A change may be part of a programme of continuous improvement, in which what are often small-scale changes are made to the way things are done, with the ultimate aim of improving the quality of products or services. Or a change may be a one-off, possibly large-scale project, planned by senior management. Either way, you, as a first line manager, are likely to be involved as an instigator of change, as one who encourages others to instigate change, and as one who has to lead and inspire others in implementing change planned by others.

In this workbook we will look at the forces behind change, both in the general environment and within your organization, and the opportunities and threats they can present to both your organization and your team. We will look at how you can describe the changes taking place and assess their costs and benefits, and plan their introduction. More than anything else, as a leader of change, you must have the skills necessary to convince others of its benefits – skills that this workbook aims to help you develop.

4.1 Objectives

When you have completed this workbook you will be better able to:

- identify the forces behind change, and how they might affect your organization or department;
- recognize the beneficial aspects of change, whether it be through continuous improvement or through one-off projects;

- initiate improvements in workplace activities;
- describe the effect of change on systems and procedures and assess the costs and benefits of change;
- plan change projects.

5 Activity planner

The following Activities require some planning so you may want to look at these now.

- Activities 6, 8 and 11, on pages 10, 13 and 17, ask you – perhaps with the help of your manager and colleagues – to identify factors in the general environment that could act as forces for change within your organization or department.
- Activity 14, on page 21, asks you – perhaps with the help of your manager and colleagues – to identify your organization's strengths and weaknesses.

Some or all of these Activities may provide the basis of evidence for your S/NVQ portfolio. All Portfolio Activities and the Work-based assignments are posted with this icon.

The icon states the elements to which the Portfolio Activities and Work-based assignment relate.

The Work-based assignment, on page 94, suggests that you discuss with three workteam members or colleagues their experience of change. You might like to start thinking about whom you should approach, and perhaps arrange a time to have a chat with them.

Session A
External forces for change

1 Introduction

If, in the 1950s, you had asked someone whether change was unusual – a disruption to the everyday routine – the chances are that they would have said 'yes'. During the 1950s people talked about 'having a steady job', and many jobs followed a predictable routine. Of course, changes did take place – organizations moved premises, people were promoted, new product lines were introduced and so on. But these could be identified as departures from the 'normal' established pattern, to which everyone would return as soon as possible.

The situation today is very different. In all walks of life, in all trades and professions, it is very difficult to define normality. It has become 'normal' to expect regular announcements about the following.

- Mergers and takeovers.
  If we want to keep up with 'who owns whom' we must be keen students of the financial press. (Is your local electricity company now under German control? Or is it part of the same organization that delivers your water?)
- Businesses closing down or opening up.
  These result in many redundancies on the one hand or many new jobs on the other.
- Political and economic changes, affecting millions of people.
  The process of globalization, in which multinational corporations move their operations around the world and individuals travel and communicate with one another across frontiers with ease, means that events in one country can immediately affect people in other countries as never before.

Nowadays, the only thing you can say with certainty about your job is that it will change!

1

■ Technological advances.
Many – of which the Internet is just one obvious example – promise (or threaten) to make us revise our ways of working.

Apart from these large-scale changes, we have to deal with local events that are just as important to us. It doesn't seem helpful to try to identify what is normal because in a very real sense, change is the norm.

2 Categorizing forces for change

Think about almost any aspect of your life – your home, your workplace, where you shop and bank, where you spend your leisure time – and you will be able to identify something that has changed in the last few years.

Activity 1

Identify one change that has occurred in the last few years in each of the following areas.

■ Your home

_____

_____

■ Your workplace

_____

_____

■ Your nearest town

_____

_____

- The country as a whole

_____

_____

There are, of course, numerous things that you could have written down, depending on your particular situation. But to get an idea of the variety of changes that have occurred, let's consider Janice's situation.

A mother of two teenage children, Janice works as the supervisor of the meat and fish counter in her local supermarket. At home she and her husband have recently bought a high-powered computer in response to the demands of her children, who like to spend many hours each week on the Internet. They have also recently bought a DVD player and a digital TV. Now she and her husband are considering borrowing £8,000 to buy a new car because interest rates are so much lower than they were a few years ago. Janice has no financial worries, but she is concerned about her children, one of whom struggles to cope with the growing number of public exams.

At work, Janice is spending more and more time overseeing the packaging of orders for items purchased by customers on-line. She has also had to start looking at new types of fish to order up as stocks of some of the old favourites, such as cod, have diminished and become more expensive. In the past she often drove into town from her house in the suburbs. However, the local council has now created a network of bus and cycle lanes, and made parking much more expensive, so it is easier and cheaper to go by bus. One of the things she regularly enjoys during a shopping trip is a cappuccino in one of the many new coffee bars that have opened up all over town. Always keen on going to the cinema, she now has a wide choice of films every week as two of the local cinemas have become eight-screen complexes.

For her annual holiday she always goes abroad. Flights are so cheap that the whole family has been able to go to Florida twice in the last few years. Whenever she goes away in Britain she is appalled by how much time they spend sitting in traffic jams on the motorway. On the other hand, there are a few resorts on the south coast that she is fond of visiting because they have become 'continental' in feel, with pubs, cafes and restaurants open and selling alcohol all day, and setting up tables and chairs on the pavement. She can remember the time when it was difficult to have a glass of wine in the afternoon because of the licensing laws.

Activity 2

A variety of factors have brought about changes in Janice's life in the last few years. These can be divided into a number of categories, such as political, economic, social, technological, legal or environmental. Try to identify one factor in each category that has brought about change in Janice's life – or the life of her family.

■ Political

_____

_____

■ Economic

_____

_____

■ Social

_____

_____

■ Technological

_____

_____

■ Legal

_____

_____

■ Environmental

_____

_____

To identify political factors that can bring change in your life, you need to consider what new policies have been introduced by the government. In Janice's case, the government's introduction since the 1990s of numerous public exams for children, such as National Curriculum Assessments, is one political factor that has a direct impact on her family's life.

A major economic factor that has affected Janice's life is the drop in interest rates. Social factors include various changes in the leisure sector, such as cinemas becoming multi-screen complexes and an increasing number of coffee bars serving up Italian-style coffee. Technological factors include the ever-changing capabilities of personal computers and the introduction of digital TV. Legal factors include various changes in the licensing laws, which from 1988 allowed all-day opening of pubs in England and Wales and made it possible to buy an alcoholic drink any time of the day.

Finally, there are the environmental factors. For Janice, these include the introduction of bus and cycle lanes in an attempt by the local council to cut down on pollution by cars. There is also the fact that over-fishing has had a major impact on stocks of popular fish such as cod, causing the European Commission to impose strict quotas and forcing retailers to find other fish to sell – so bringing about change in Janice's job.

All the factors that have caused change in Janice's life will have had an effect on various organizations, from exam boards to bus companies, supermarkets, pubs, restaurants, cinema chains, and so on. If such organizations do not make a point of scanning the general environment for changes that could well have an impact on them, their business will ultimately suffer. As a manager you can play a part in identifying these external forces for change – and become aware of developments that may have an effect on your job and the jobs of your team – by carrying out what is known as a PESTLE analysis. (PESTLE is an acronym derived from the words: political, economic, social, technological, legal and environmental.)

It's worth bearing in mind that it's not always easy to isolate one type of factor from another – many political factors are also economic, for example. And, in fact, this doesn't really matter. The main purpose of doing a PESTLE analysis is to get you thinking about what is happening in the external environment, and what changes you, your team and your organization should consider making in response.

Activity 3

Read through the following two examples of change. As you read them make a note of the types of factors that brought about the change. Were they political, economic, social, technological, legal or environmental? Briefly explain the reasons for your answer in each case.

Example 1

Caroline Quigley has been a clerk at the old-established firm of Terence Gratton Ltd for more than twenty years. Until about ten years ago, she would have described her job as 'mostly paperwork'. Then the company computerized nearly all clerical functions, and Caroline had to learn to work at a keyboard, and to produce results using a complex customized accounting package. It was a difficult period of adjustment, but now she couldn't imagine going back to the old ways.

However, as Caroline had discovered, it wasn't a simple question of learning a set of procedures and putting them into practice. The organization has been branching into new areas of business and its customer base is continuously changing. In addition, the software company that provided the computer package is regularly updating the system and the equipment has already been upgraded three times.

When she thinks about it, Caroline is surprised by how well she has coped with it all. She had once been 'computer illiterate', but others in the office now look to her for expert help.

Example 2

Robertson's was the only second-hand bookshop in the Highfields area of Busbury and brought its owner, Tom, a steady but unspectacular income. When another second-hand bookshop opened up just down the road, Tom wasn't worried at first as he felt his shop had many unique features that would continue to attract the customers. He was well-known for his large sections on the cinema, theatre and art. Furthermore, he was always being told by customers how much they appreciated the detailed knowledge he and his assistant had of their stock. Several customers had actually written to say that they had been delighted that he had managed to track down a particular book they wanted at another bookseller's.

Unfortunately for Tom, his competitor down the road, Meera, had taken a good look at Robertson's and come to the conclusion that while Robertson's had a really good selection, many of the books were overpriced. The thing to do was to set up a bargain section in which books were offered at prices that undercut those at Robertson's. Meera was also well aware that many second-hand bookshops were beginning to struggle as a result of competition from dealers selling books on the Internet. She decided that the best way to cope with this was to acquire a computer herself and start selling her more valuable books on the Internet herself. She already had some basic computer skills – she just needed to brush up on creating a database. Once she had got her toe in the market using a Website with which many bookshops were registered, she might even consider setting up her own Website.

Much as Tom's customers appreciated the service they got in his shop, many of them appreciated Meera's prices even more. However, Meera doubted if this would have been enough to keep her in business if she had not decided to start selling on the Internet. She entered titles in the database whenever she had a spare moment, and she was amazed at how her sales began to increase dramatically, every day Tom saw her setting off to the post office with a pile of parcels to send to customers while he fretted over his declining till receipts. She had told him about her success with the Internet but he didn't see how he could follow suit as he and his assistant knew nothing about computers. Within a year Tom' shop was doing only half the trade it had before. Increasingly demoralized by the lack of customers, and approaching an age when he could retire, he decided that he had no alternative but to close down.

Example 1

Change factors

_____

Reasons for answer

_____

_____

Example 2

Change factors

_____

Reasons for answer

_____

_____

So what conclusions did you come to about the types of factors that produced change in the two examples? In Caroline Quigley's case, there was certainly technology involved, as computerization only comes through advances in technology. But the investment in technology was part of the company's efforts to stay efficient, and to keep up with a changing marketplace. You might have decided that the root cause of the changes was an economic one.

In Tom Robertson's case, the closure of the shop seems to have been brought about by competition, which is an economic force. But there were social and technological forces at work, too. His competitor, Meera, doubted whether she could have stayed in business without her Internet sales. The demand among local customers for ordinary second-hand books seemed to be going down at the same time as the Internet made it possible to sell the rarer and more valuable books to customers throughout the world.

As even these two examples show, more than one factor is generally at work in creating the need for change. And in the case of businesses that have to make a profit, one of these factors will almost certainly be economic.

3 Political, economic and social factors

Unless you keep up-to-date with the news, you may not always be aware of many political, economic and social developments. All can have a major impact on you and your team.

3.1 Political factors

The government in power, and the policies that the government pursues, can have a major impact on organizations. A government decision, for example, to have low inflation as a chief goal results in interest rates being set low, which in turn means that people are happy to borrow more and spend more in the shops. They are also prepared to spend a lot more on housing, which means an increase in business for estate agents, banks and building societies.

Returning to the example of increasing the number of public examinations for school children: by 2002 children had up to 87 official tests in their school careers. As a result, there has been a huge expansion of business for the organizations responsible for the setting and marking of examination papers – all the result of political changes.

3.2 Economic factors

Some developments in the economy are dictated by government policies, notably measures announced in the annual budget, such as a cut in corporation tax for small businesses, or an increase in employers' national insurance contributions.

Other economic developments have nothing to do with the government. The destruction of New York's World Trade Center on 11 September 2001 by two planes that had been hijacked by terrorists had major worldwide effects. One example was the downturn in the demand for airline tickets. This, in turn, meant that a few airlines, such as Swissair, actually went out of business, while others, such as British Airways, had to reduce the number of flights and routes on which they operated as their profits slumped in the period that followed.

Quite apart from economic pressures created by governments and world events, there are those to which most organizations have to react in the course of a year.

Activity 4

4 mins

Jot down two or three economic pressures to which most organizations may have to react in the course of a year.

_____

_____

_____

_____

_____

You could have listed the following:

■ the pressure of competition – to compete with their rivals, companies have to try to make their products or services more attractive in some way, so as to retain or increase their share of the market;
■ pressure from shareholders, who demand high profits and dividends;
■ pressure from financial institutions, who lend the money organizations need for investment, but who demand interest and prompt payment.

3.3 Social factors

Social factors may be long-term or fleeting. Among long-term factors are changes in the age profile and ethnic composition of the population. As people live longer, the percentage of people over the age of 50 is increasing considerably, and more and more businesses are now considering how to address their needs. This particularly applies to people who have retired early, have a good pension and lots of leisure time.

Among the more fleeting social factors are fashions in clothes. What has been popular in the past is no indicator of what people will buy in the future. The shape of jeans or the length of skirts, for example, changes from year to year.

Activity 5

What other short-term social changes can you think of, apart from fashions in clothes? Jot down two or three.

_____

_____

_____

Look at a guide to TV programmes for the coming week and you'll be able to spot areas in which short-term change is the norm. You will probably find lots of programmes about house décor, revealing what colours, materials and styles of furniture are fashionable. Food and wine is also a common subject. Sun-dried tomatoes, goats' cheese, rocket salad and chardonnay wines all became popular items in bistro-style restaurants in the 1990s. What items will replace them in the next decade? There has also been a massive increase in the number of programmes in which groups of people are brought together in sometimes difficult situations and are then the subject of constant filming. 'Big Brother' is a famous example, but there have been many others. You have probably thought of many other forms of entertainment that have changed considerably in the last decade.

Activity 6

S/NVQ C5

This Activity may provide the basis of appropriate evidence for your S/NVQ portfolio. If you are intending to take this course of action, it might be better to write your answer on separate sheets of paper.

Are there any political, economic and social factors that you think your organization or, if you work for a large organization, your department should take account of in the near future? (You may find it helpful to talk to your manager and colleagues about this.) Note down what they are and what effect they could have on your organization if it did not make any changes in response to these factors.

Political factors

_____

_____

Possible effects

_____

_____

Economic factors

_____

_____

Possible effects

_____

_____

Social factors

_____

_____

Possible effects

_____

_____

You may have found this Activity quite difficult. If so, you should think about ways in which you can keep up-to-date with the full range of developments that may affect your organization or department in the future. These include:

- reading journals and newspapers;
- taking to suppliers' representatives;
- reading company newsletters and bulletins;
- attending management briefings;
- going on relevant courses;
- talking to colleagues in other parts of the organization, and in other organizations.

4 Technological factors

A great many changes that take place at work are driven by developments in technology. If we go back in history, the most fundamental change in working life in Britain came about as a result of the invention of machines such as the spinning jenny and the steam engine in the second half of the eighteenth century. Before this Industrial Revolution, most people worked on the land or in cottage industries – in 1750, only about 20% of England's population lived in towns. After this date there was a vast increase in the number of people toiling in factories and coalfields and by 1850 over 50% lived in towns.

Now we seem to be coming full circle, as many more of the population are working from home or in small businesses. Technology is a major factor in the change. The post-industrial revolution is with us: only about 20% of workers in Britain are employed by manufacturing companies, and most coal mines have been closed.

But who can say whether this will be the picture in 20 or 30 years' time?

Activity 7

3 mins

Apart from the computer, what inventions in the 20th and 21st centuries have changed, or are in the process of changing, the way people work? Jot down two or three.

_____

_____

_____

You might have mentioned:

■ various forms of transport, such as cars, aeroplanes and high-speed trains;
■ space technology;
■ modern telecommunications, including permanent and mobile phones, and satellite links;
■ the Internet;

- automation and industrial robots;
- modern fabrics;

or a hundred other inventions.

It is clear that technology is changing all our lives and promises to alter them even more in the future.

Activity 8

5 mins

S/NVQ C5

This Activity may provide the basis of appropriate evidence for your S/NVQ portfolio. If you are intending to take this course of action, it might be better to write your answer on separate sheets of paper.

Make a note of two or more ways in which you anticipate your job, and the jobs of your team, may be changed within the next few years as a result of new technological changes. (You may find it helpful to talk to your manager and colleagues about this.)

_____

_____

_____

_____

_____

We can all speculate about what might happen in the future, but it is more useful to base your predictions on known facts. For example, if you use plastics, are you aware of developments in the chemical industry, where new kinds of plastics are being tested? Or if you work in building, you may have heard about new materials or processes, which may outdate existing practices. Most kinds of work are likely to change in the future as a result of new technology.

Remember: wise managers make it their business to keep a close watch on changing events in their own industry, whatever the causes.

5 Legal factors

Laws and regulations affect employment in many ways. For example, the law has brought about changes, generally for the better, in working practices. In 1842, a law was passed forbidding the employment of children under ten years of age in coal mines. At that time workers had virtually no rights. Today the working population is protected in a number of ways, through a series of Acts of Parliament.

This is one area of law – employee protection law.

Other kinds of law which affect the workplace include:

■ health and safety, law;
■ laws governing the conduct of unions;
■ contract law;
■ insurance law;
■ consumer protection law;
■ laws controlling the carriage of goods;
■ company law, which deals with the registration of companies and the auditing of company finances.

Activity 9

Can you think of any laws or regulations in the last decade or so that have forced organizations to introduce change – either in the way they treat their staff, in the processes they employ, or in the products or services they provide? Jot down a couple of examples.

_____

_____

_____

_____

One comparatively recent example of a law that has affected conditions for staff is the introduction of the minimum wage in 1999. Before its introduction many organizations protested about it and said that it would cause job losses and even put some of them out of business. In fact, it had none of the feared effects.

As far as products are concerned, among the legal measures that have produced change are those banning the use of leaded petrol (in 2000) and the use of ozone-depleting chlorofluorocarbons (CFCs) in fridges and aerosols (in 1995). Both reflect a growing concern with the effect we are having on the environment. This brings us to the next set of factors that contribute to change.

6 Environmental factors

Scientists don't all agree about many questions on the environment. But you don't have to be a 'green' to admit that there has been a significant change in public awareness of these issues.

Since the 1980s there has been ever-increasing concern about the effect of human activities on the environment. There are two main environmental issues.

- The Earth and its atmosphere do not have an unlimited capacity to cope with the many forms of pollution associated with industrialization.
- The Earth does not have unlimited resources for the world's population to exploit and destroy.

6.1 Pollution

Industrial pollution has been a problem in Britain since the 19th century. The terrible smogs that engulfed London in 1952, killing hundreds, showed just how much damage could be done by pollution. In this case the pollution was caused by smoke from burning coal.

It's now known that one of the effects of atmospheric pollution is the depletion of the ozone layer. This layer of ozone filters the sun's rays, and protects us from over-exposure to the ultra-violet radiation. If the layer were to disappear completely we would all be dead. Its loss is blamed on substances produced by industrial processes. Chemicals called chlorofluorocarbons (CFCs), traditionally used in refrigerators and aerosols, have been identified as being partly to blame. It has been proved that CFCs react in the atmosphere with ultra-violet radiation to form chlorine. This results in the ozone being converted to oxygen. Governments and manufacturers have been forced to respond to this threat. In many countries there has been a ban since 1995 on the use of CFCs in the production of goods – though there are still many old fridges around containing CFCs.

Another major environmental problem that you will have heard about is global warming. A layer of carbon dioxide in the Earth's atmosphere traps heat from the sun's rays in a naturally occurring process known as the 'greenhouse effect'. It is now generally believed that this greenhouse effect has been increased by the emission of carbon dioxide from the burning of fossil fuels, such as coal and oil, leading to a rise in the Earth's average temperature. The effect could be the melting of ice throughout the world, a rise in the level of the world's oceans, and the flooding of low-lying areas. Governments have responded by attempting to reach agreement on cutting carbon dioxide emissions. This has affected many industries. In Britain, for example, gas has largely replaced coal as the fuel burnt in the production of electricity, and there are now very few coal mines still operating.

6.2 Finite resources

Contributing to the increase in the amount of carbon dioxide in the atmosphere is the destruction of the world's forests. Trees (which absorb carbon dioxide) are among the Earth's finite resources and there is an ongoing campaign in many countries to stop them disappearing. There is also a campaign to stop the extinction of many species of plants and animals. It would be hard to imagine 50 years ago that cod would one day be in danger of becoming extinct as a result of over-fishing.

A development that represents a threat to some organizations can represent an opportunity to others.

Hand-in-hand with efforts to stop the dangerous depletion of various resources and to cut down on the amount of pollution are efforts to recycle as much as possible. All organizations in Britain now have to abide by regulations on the production and recycling of waste. Others have taken advantage of the public's concern over what we are doing to the environment and now produce goods that use natural resources. They may also be sold in recyclable packaging. The Body Shop and its competitors, such as Aveda and Origins, are obvious examples.

The success of businesses such as The Body Shop reflects growing public concern over what we are doing to the environment. This concern is reflected in the products and services that some organizations offer.

Activity 10 ·

In your local shops or supermarket you will almost certainly find a number of products that reflect public concern with environmental issues. Write down the names of two or three of these products and how they reflect this concern.

_____

_____

_____

Most supermarkets now sell organic products in response to growing unease about the effect modern farming techniques are having on the land, on animals, and on our health. The campaign against genetically modified (GM) foods, and the refusal of many people to buy them, also partly reflects concern about the effects of GM crops on the natural environment. The problem of CFCs has resulted in sprays that are CFC-free and in cleaning products with ingredients that will not harm the environment.

There are many other examples that you may have thought of.

Activity 11 ·

S/NVQ C5

This Activity may provide the basis of appropriate evidence for your S/NVQ portfolio. If you are intending to take this course of action, it might be better to write your answer on separate sheets of paper.

Are there any legal and/or environmental factors that you think your organization or department should take account of in the near future? What are they and what effect they could have on your organization if it did not make any changes in response to these factors? (Again you may find it helpful to talk to your manager and colleagues about this.)

_____

_____

_____

_____

_____

7 Recognizing opportunities and threats

You may remember that in Section 3 we considered the example of Tom Robertson's second-hand bookshop. The business came under threat when another bookshop opened up down the road selling many titles at lower prices than those charged by Tom. Tom's rival, Meera, then increased her profits and made her position more secure by starting to sell her more valuable books on the Internet. Tom's response was eventually to give up and go out of business. But Tom could have decided to seize his opportunities and actually compete. He, too, could have used the Web to sell his more valuable books. He had an excellent stock so there was a good chance that taking this route could have saved his business.

A particular set of changes in the external environment can represent both threats and opportunities for an organization. Ovaltine, a malt and egg powder drink stopped being manufactured in Britain in 2002. Marketed as a drink that is both good for you and helps to put you to sleep, it lost its appeal in a society where people lead increasingly busy lives and want drinks and snacks to keep them going rather than knock them out. Ironically, the original Swiss version of Ovaltine was renowned for its ability to increase energy and was the official drink at the 1948 Olympics. But the manufacturers of Ovaltine failed to capitalize on this while other soft drink manufacturers, such as Lucozade, responded to the growing demand for drinks that give energy and can act as an indispensable aid for anyone doing a sport.

Activity 12

5 mins

S/NVQ
C5

This Activity may provide the basis of appropriate evidence for your S/NVQ portfolio. If you are intending to take this course of action, it might be better to write your answer on separate sheets of paper.

Look back at Activities 6, 8 and 11, in which you identified a range of factors that might have an effect on your organization or department. Do any of these represent threats to your organization? Do any represent opportunities? (Remember the same factors can be both threats and opportunities.) Make a note of any opportunities and threats that you identify.

Opportunities

_____

_____

Threats

_____

_____

 # 8 Strengths and weaknesses

Whether your, or any other organization, is actually capable of responding to the threats and taking advantage of the opportunities will depend on its strengths and weaknesses.

These will include:

- the things it does well or badly;
- its resources or lack of them in certain areas;
- it staff skills or gaps in these skills;
- the high or low staff morale;
- the high or low demand for its products or services;
- its strong or weak financial situation.

Activity 13

Returning to the example of Tom Robertson's bookshop, on the basis of the information you've received so far, what would you say were its main strengths and weaknesses?

Strengths

_____

_____

_____

Weaknesses

_____

_____

_____

Among the strengths of Tom Robertson's bookshop were its large, well-organized sections on subjects, such as cinema, theatre and art, not covered in much depth by rival bookshops. Tom and his assistant also had a detailed knowledge of their stock and were always more than willing to help customers find the book they want. If they didn't have it themselves they would discover a bookseller somewhere in the country who did.

On the other hand, the business had several weaknesses. Tom generally over priced the more ordinary second-hand books. He and his assistant were feeling increasingly demoralized by the lack of customers on some days. In fact, there were some weeks when the shop barely took enough to cover all the outgoings. They had heard about the success of their rival down the road in doing business on the Internet, but neither of them had any computer skills.

Activity 14

S/NVQ
C5

This Activity may provide the basis of appropriate evidence for your S/NVQ portfolio. If you are intending to take this course of action, it might be better to write your answer on separate sheets of paper.

You might find it helpful to discuss the questions in this Activity with your manager and colleagues.

What are your organization's or department's strengths? Consider the following questions and jot down any strengths you can identify below.

- ■ What does it do well?
- ■ What resources does it have?
- ■ What skills do its staff have?
- ■ Is staff morale high?
- ■ Is there a high demand for its products or services?
- ■ Is it in a strong financial situation?

_____

_____

_____

_____

What are your organization's or department's weaknesses? Consider the following questions and jot down any weaknesses you can identify below.

- ■ What does it do badly?
- ■ What resources does it lack?
- ■ What are the gaps in the skills of its staff?
- ■ Is staff morale low?
- ■ Is there only a low demand for its products or services?
- ■ Is it in a weak financial situation?

_____

_____

_____

_____

9 Putting it all together: SWOT analysis

In identifying your organization's strengths and weaknesses, and the opportunities and threats presented by the external environment, you have in effect carried out what is called a **SWOT** analysis. This can act as a springboard for change, helping managers to understand the nature of the organization they are working for and identify ways of moving forward in the future.

A SWOT analysis is usually set out in a box divided into four sections, as in the example below.

SWOT analysis for Tom Robertson's Bookshop

Strengths	Weaknesses
■ Well-organized and extensive sections on cinema, theatre and art ■ Staff have detailed knowledge of stock ■ Able and willing to locate books held by other booksellers	■ Ordinary books perhaps priced too high ■ Demoralized staff ■ Staff lack computer skills ■ Low and declining profits/little capital
Opportunities	Threats
■ Can sell more valuable books on Internet	■ Nearby competitor selling books at lower prices ■ Declining market for ordinary second-hand books

Looking at this SWOT analysis it is clear that Tom Robertson needed to start capitalizing on his excellent sections on cinema, theatre and art, and start selling on the Internet. It is also clear that there were various weaknesses he should have addressed, such as the prices of his ordinary books and his, and his assistant's, lack of computer skills. Although he had little capital, he could have considered borrowing enough to buy a computer and pay for a computer skills course. This would have been a major change for Tom, but was necessary if he was to stay in business.

Activity 15 ·

10 mins

S/NVQ
C5

This Activity may provide the basis of appropriate evidence for your S/NVQ portfolio. If you are intending to take this course of action, it might be better to write your answer on separate sheets of paper.

Try doing a SWOT analysis for your organization or department. As preparation, first look over your answers to Activities 12 and 14.

Strengths	Weaknesses
Opportunities	Threats

Once you have done a SWOT analysis you may be able to make some suggestions on what changes your organization can make to:

- build on its strengths;
- rectify its weaknesses;
- grasp opportunities;
- overcome threats.

Activity 16 ·

8 mins

S/NVQ
C5

This Activity may provide the basis of appropriate evidence for your S/NVQ portfolio. If you are intending to take this course of action, it might be better to write your answer on separate sheets of paper.

Looking at your SWOT analysis, what suggestions do you have for change in your organization or department?

_____

_____

_____

_____

Scanning the general environment outside your organization will at least enable you to keep abreast of developments so you won't be taken by surprise when they lead to change for you and your team. Better still, it may give you ideas on new directions or new ways of doing things for your team, and so help you to have a proactive role in change.

Self-assessment I · 15 mins

1 What categories of factors that can act as forces for change does PESTLE stand for? Put a tick against the correct answer.

a Political, Ethical, Social, Technological, Legal and Environmental

b Political, Economic, Social, Technological, Legal and Ethical

c Political, Economic, Social, Technological, Legal and Environmental

d Political, Economic, Social, Technological, Legal and Epidemiological

2 Complete each of the following sentences with one of the words from the PESTLE acronym.

a Pressures created by financial institutions, as well as governments and world events, contribute to _____ factors.

b _____ factors may be long-term or fleeting. Among the long-term factors are changes in the composition of the population.

c The policies pursued by government help to shape _____ factors.

d Consumer protection laws are among the _____ factors.

e Among _____ factors is the issue of finite resources.

f Numerous inventions that have changed the way people work are among the _____ factors.

3 Fill each of the gaps in the following sentences with one of the words from the SWOT acronym.

Among an organization's _____ are the things it does well and the skills of its staff. Among an organization's _____ are the gaps in staff skills. _____ are those things in the environment that an organization must overcome. _____ are those things an organization should grasp if it is to develop and prosper.

4 As a manager you need to keep up-to-date with developments that may affect your organization in the future. Name three ways in which you can do this.

_____

_____

_____

5 Which of the following two sentences do you think is most correct? Briefly explain the reason for your choice.

a Increasing concern about environmental issues can only represent a threat to organizations.

b Increasing concern about environmental issues can represent an opportunity for some organizations.

The most correct statement is _____ because:

_____

_____

_____

Answers to these questions can be found on page 103.

10 Summary

- Nowadays change is not a disruption of normality: in a very real sense, change is the norm.

- Forces in the general environment that lead to change in organizations can be categorized as:

  - political factors
  - Economic factors
  - Social factors
  - Technological factors
  - Legal factors
  - Environmental factors

- Carrying out a PESTLE analysis will help you to identify the external forces for change that may affect your organization and your department in the future.

- You can keep up-to-date with developments that may affect your department by:

  - reading journals and newspapers;
  - talking to suppliers' representatives;
  - reading company newsletters and bulletins;
  - attending management briefings;
  - going on relevant courses;
  - talking to colleagues in your own and other organizations.

- By carrying out a SWOT analysis for an organization (or department) you identify the following.

  - Strengths
  - Weaknesses
  - Opportunities
  - Threats

- An organization's strengths and weaknesses are internal factors. They include:

  - the things it does well or badly;
  - its resources or lack of them in certain areas;
  - its staff skills or gaps in these skills;
  - the high or low staff morale;
  - the high or low demand for its products or services;
  - its strong or weak financial position.

- The opportunities and threats are presented by the external environment.

- Carrying out a SWOT analysis should enable you to identify ways in which an organization, or department, can:

  - build on its strengths;
  - rectify its weaknesses;
  - grasp opportunities;
  - overcome threats.

Session B
Continuous improvement and change

1 Introduction

In the last session you identified some changes that your organization might make in response to a range of external factors. It's almost certain that among these external factors will be particular needs and wants of customers – both actual and potential. If Tom Robertson (our bookseller from Session A) had started to sell his books on the Internet, he would have been responding to the need of customers to be able to order rare second-hand books from book-sellers anywhere in the world.

In many ways Tom Robertson offered a quality service to his customers. For example, he was always happy to find any book they wanted, whether it be in his shop or with another bookseller. And yet his business declined, at least partly because the prices he was charging were too high compared with those of his main competitor. He had not understood that providing a quality service or product means meeting the needs of customers at prices they can afford.

In today's highly competitive world, even this does not necessarily guarantee that an organization will succeed. It should aim to go further than this and con-tinuously improve its products and services so that they meet, and eventually exceed, customer needs.

Continuous improvement means constant, but also gradual, change, as you will see in this session.

2 What does continuous improvement involve?

The idea that organizations should aim to improve the quality of their products and services on a continuous basis was first taken up in Japan, where the word for continuous improvement is 'kaizen'. It comes from a book published in 1986 entitled *Kaizen: The Key to Japan's Competitive Success*, written by Masaaki Imai.

2.1 Kaizen

EXTENSION 1
In this workbook we will look at a small selection of kaizen tools. An excellent source of more information on kaizen is Extension 1, *Kaizen strategies for successful organisational change*, by Michael Colenso. You will find more information on Extension 1 on page 102.

At the heart of kaizen is the idea that if customers' constantly changing needs and wants are to be met, there must be continuous improvement in small steps, at all levels, forever. Everyone has a role to play in achieving it, from senior management down to first line managers and their staff. Senior and middle managers need to concentrate on establishing the necessary strategy, structures and systems, and on monitoring what is being achieved. First line managers, on the other hand, need to concentrate on encouraging staff to come up with suggestions for improvements and ensure that these are responded to. This of course means that staff must come up with suggestions and be prepared to change the way they do things and acquire new skills.

Activity 16 · 5 mins

1   What ideas, if any, have you had in the last week or so for improvements in the workplace? Jot down one or two, no matter how small you think they are.

_____

_____

_____

_____

2   What ideas have your staff had? Again, jot down one or two.

_____

_____

_____

_____

There are all sorts of things you could have written here, but the chances are that they were to do with one of the following:

- **the physical conditions in which you and your staff work**
  These include the layout of your workplace, and environmental factors such as noise, lighting, temperature and ventilation.

- **the resources you and your staff work with**
  Resources can range from money, to equipment, machines, tools, vehicles, materials, information and people.

- **the relationships you have with other people, both within and outside the organization**
  'Other people' can include suppliers, customers, colleagues, the people you manage, and managers at higher levels than yours.

- **the procedures you and your staff follow**
  For each part of your job there will be particular step-by-step procedures you are supposed to follow – or there may be a marked absence of procedures. Established procedures are not always the best, and a lack of any agreed procedure can sometimes result in chaos.

Activity 17

3 mins

Have a look at the ideas for improvements you jotted down in Activity 1. Try putting each one into one of the four categories listed below.

Physical conditions

_____

Relationships

_____

Resources

_____

Procedures

_____

Here's an example of how one manager's job can generate numerous ideas for improvement in all four categories.

Uma is the Publications Officer for a medium-sized charity. Among her responsibilities is the production of a bi-monthly, four-page newsletter for staff and regular contributors. It is only a small item, but it takes up far too much of her time, diverting her attention from her other responsibilities, which range from producing press releases to organizing the editing, design and printing of training packs. One of the two editors who work for her, Sam, has the job of getting all the material together to pass on to an external designer. This not only includes text from contributors within the organization, many of whom seem to have no idea about deadlines, but also photos the quality of which the designer often complains about.

All too often Sam gets into a panic over the need to meet the design and printing schedule and has to turn to Uma for help. Not only this, but he distracts the other editor, Gemma, from what she is doing. She sits right next to him and can't help but listen in to his harassed-sounding phone calls and then take a look at what he is doing, either on the screen of his word-processor or on the manuscript or proofs lying on the small clear space on his desk or, more usually, on the floor.

When Uma looks at this situation she can see a range of ways in which it could be improved. Starting with physical conditions, it's clear that having Sam and Gemma sitting right next to each other is not the best layout for their office. They need to consider how they can make better use of the available space, while at the same time ensuring that both of them get sufficient light.

In terms of resources, Sam has all the basic computer equipment he needs, but he is short of something very basic: desk space. When they consider how best to rearrange the office they will also need to consider the possibility of changing some of the fittings and furniture. Another resource they are missing is a good digital camera. The quality of the photos they pass on to the designer is poor because they are often taken by people, Sam included, at a low resolution on cheap digital cameras.

Then there is the thorny problem of relationships. Sam's relationship with both Gemma and Uma is being affected by the fact that he often becomes irritable when he's under pressure. This could be sorted out if the pressures on him were reduced. One of the most obvious things that causes this pressure is the late arrival of contributions to the newsletter – particularly those from senior managers – and the tendency of people to start changing what they have written when they see it on designed pages. A new relationship needs to be established with senior managers, in which they recognize the need to show more consideration to Sam and the Publications Department as a whole. Perhaps they don't even realize what problems they are causing, because the Publications Department doesn't make it clear what it wants.

Finally, there are the procedures they follow. It is obviously not an effective way of putting the newsletter together to have people sending in contributions later than the schedule agreed with the designer, and then – in the general haste to get the newsletter underway – passing on these contributions without editing them properly or cutting them down to roughly the required length.

If Uma was able to make all the improvements that she has identified as necessary, she would be on the way to establishing a really effective process. It would not, however, be a perfect process. In kaizen, there is always room for improvement.

2.2 Process improvement

Let's have another look at Uma's situation and focus on the procedures that are followed in the production of the newsletter. If she can sort these out, she will be well on the way to making the overall process effective.

At the moment, the week after a newsletter is distributed to staff:

- an email goes out to everyone asking them to submit features, and dates for the 'diary section' for the next newsletter by a date no later than four weeks' time;
- Uma approaches one or more members of staff to ask if they will write a short feature on one of the subjects she knows to be of particular interest at present;
- Sam begins collecting a dossier of items for the News section.

The first major problem is that not all the promised material arrives by the date it is due. The second is that if, and when, it does arrive it is often way over the agreed length and requires major cutting – which in turn means the material going backwards and forwards between the contributor and Sam. Over the course of the week before everything is due to go off to the designer, Sam battles away on his computer to get the material edited and cut to approximately the number of words needed to fill four pages. Because it arrives in bits he has to do this between other tasks. He also often doesn't know what pictures are going to be included and so can't take them into account in his estimated word counts. Inevitably, not all the material goes off to the designer at the same time.

The designer does the best he can with what he's been given. However, when the final bits of text finally arrive, some of it only roughly edited because it's so late, he invariably has to change the layout of one or more pages. There's also the problem with the pictures. These usually come from a number of people, none of whom have the right equipment to take a picture that will reproduce well. This means a lot of phone calls to see if something better can be supplied.

Eventually, the designer gets the newsletter to the stage where proofs can be sent to Sam, Uma and all contributors for their approval. Unfortunately, it's often at this stage that contributors decide they want to totally rewrite something, and Sam and Uma start doing some serious editing. In theory, Uma's only involvement should be to give the newsletter a final check, but she's found too many mistakes in printed newsletters in the past not to get more heavily involved. The net result of all this is that a large number of corrections go back to the designer. Inevitably, mistakes are made in the correction process, and sometimes Sam ends up having to check three or four proofs, often outside official working hours as the deadline approaches for getting the newsletter to the printer.

All this is a huge waste of time and energy. What can be done to eliminate this waste?

Activity 18

4 mins

Imagine you are Uma and are determined to find ways of improving the procedures for producing the newsletter. What ideas do you have? Jot down a couple.

_____

_____

_____

There are a number of things you might consider. To begin with, ideally Sam needs to get all the text on time. Uma knows that in reality it won't always be possible to get the Chief Executive, for example, to submit her contribution on time – but there is no reason why the vast majority of contributors can't do so. They need to be given more information about the various stages in the process. And they need to understand the knock-on effects of submitting text late and then deciding to rewrite it after the newsletter has been designed. Perhaps she should send out an information sheet and hold a series of brief seminars on the subject. At the same time, she could talk to them about the need to either supply high-quality pictures themselves, or be prepared to specify what pictures they would like to see included well in advance, so that Sam can arrange for good-quality pictures to be taken.

Provided Sam receives most of the text on time, he should then concentrate on editing and cutting the text to approximately the right length. If he knows what pictures are going to be included, he can work out their size on the page using a simple formula and then make a more accurate estimate of the number of words that can be fitted into the remaining space. Uma can make the whole thing easier for Sam by scheduling in a chunk of time for him to concentrate on the newsletter, and then reading through the text **before** it goes to the designer. It should then only be necessary to have three proofing stages and a minimal number of corrections – saving a lot of time for Sam, the designer and herself.

Activity 19

S/NVQ C5

This Activity may provide the basis of appropriate evidence for your S/NVQ portfolio. If you are intending to take this course of action, it might be better to write your answer on separate sheets of paper.

Identify one process in your job where you know there is a lot of room for improvement. Write down your first thoughts about the changes that should be made in terms of:

■ physical conditions:

_____

_____

■ relationships:

_____

_____

■ resources:

_____

_____

You will need your answer to Activity 19 for Activities 22, 24 and 26.

■ procedures:

_____

_____

2.3 Continuous improvement cycle

A useful model to follow in planning a programme of continuous improvement is the cycle, shown in the diagram below. It consists of:

■ doing;
■ reviewing what has been done;
■ learning from this review;
■ planning improvements on the basis of what you have learnt;
■ implementing the improvements;
■ reviewing and learning from this, and so on.

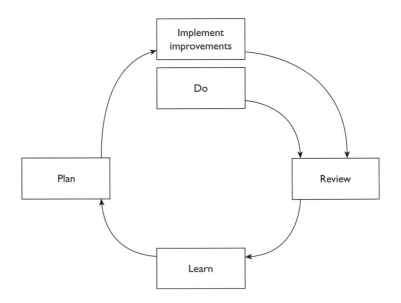

Activity 20

Below is an example of how one small incident caused a manager to use the continuous improvement cycle.

Pete is the new manager of the repro department for a printer that specializes in printing brochures and leaflets cheaply and quickly. He and his staff are responsible for 'repro', which means that they take artwork usually sent to them on disks by designers and from it produce film and then plates. One day he receives a telephone call that makes his heart sink: a client has just received proofs for a leaflet that is due to be printed that evening, in time for a conference in two days' time, and there are two mistakes on the cover, which will have to be put right. A block of text is in completely the wrong typeface and one of the pictures is missing. Correcting these mistakes is not only going to take up precious time but is also going to be costly as the printing plates will have to be remade.

How, Pete wonders, could this have happened? Why had they got almost to the point of printing the leaflet before anyone spotted the mistake? What was wrong with the processes followed by his staff – or the designer who had supplied the artwork in the first place? The first thing to do was to compare a copy of the proof with the print-out provided by the designers. This revealed that everything was as it should be on the designer's print-out, so why hadn't anyone spotted there was a problem when they produced the film that was then used to make the plates? It turned out that in their hurry to get the job done, nobody had checked the film against the print-out. If they had checked the film they would have discovered they had a problem – almost certainly because the designers had not supplied all the type fonts and images that were being used in the job. As it was, Pete was going to have to get back to the designers and get them to re-supply the artwork, thus losing valuable time. They were going to be lucky to meet the deadline for getting the leaflets printed.

It was only by paying two members of staff to do some overtime and work well into the night that Pete was able to get the leaflet printed and delivered in time for the client's conference. Once the panic was over he decided it was time to improve not only the processes followed by his staff but also those followed by the designers who supplied them with artwork. His plan was to produce:

- a checklist for designers on what must be present when supplying artwork on a disk, such as all necessary type fonts and images;
- a form for his staff listing what should be checked and signed off at each stage, which included the checking of film against the designer's print-out prior to making plates.

The checklist and form were produced and distributed. Over the next few weeks, Pete made a point of checking the forms he had given to staff to see that they were comparing film with designers' print-outs as a matter of course. He also asked the staff to help him in checking to see whether all designers were now supplying everything that was required of them and soon discovered that two of them were still getting things wrong, particularly when deadlines were tight. This was resulting in problems for everyone involved, so Pete was determined to find a way of improving the situation. He decided to send a letter to all designers, advising them to invest in some software that would automatically report on any technical faults and imperfections in a piece of artwork, and collect all the fonts and images used in the artwork.

Pete knew that this probably wouldn't be the end of the problem and that he would have to keep on reviewing the situation, but he was confident that he was on the way to not only providing a quality service to the printer's clients but also receiving a quality service from his suppliers.

■ What does the manager learn as a result of reviewing a process?

_____

_____

■ What does he or she then plan and do?

_____

_____

■ What does he or she learn as a result of an ongoing review?

_____

_____

■ What does he or she then plan and do the second time round?

_____

_____

In reviewing the processes involved in repro, Pete learnt that designers were not always supplying high-quality artwork in which all the necessary components were present, and that his own staff were not always making the necessary checks of film against designers' print-outs. He then planned to improve the process employed by both his staff and designers by preparing a checklist and form, both of which were produced and distributed. His ongoing review then revealed that two designers were still not doing all that was required of them, and so he planned to send them a letter advising them to invest in some software that would help considerably.

2.4 Being proactive in change

When things go wrong at work, it's easy to blame the staff involved. But in fact the great majority of problems are caused by defects in systems and processes.

One of the things you may have noticed in reading about Pete and the repro department is that he focused on getting processes right rather than criticizing people for their mistakes and leaving them to sort themselves out. This attitude is very much a reflection of what another American expert on quality improvement, Joseph Juran, said about the causes of problems in organizations. He stated that 85% of an organization's problems are due to systems and the processes within them, rather than to the workers involved in those processes. Processes need to be continuously changed and improved if an organization is to provide quality products and services – and who better to suggest improvements than the staff involved in the processes? The following example illustrates how one just simple suggestion for an improvement can save time and money.

> Ismail is a forklift driver on a construction site. He has worked on several sites in the past where things were in a mess, with materials lying in disorganized piles, packaging strewn all over the place, and empty forklift pallets scattered about. He is pleased to note that on this site the manager has got everything much more sorted out, and there is a place in one corner of the site for waste packaging to be collected, flattened and stacked, and for empty pallets to be stacked, each day. The only trouble is that if you happen to be working some distance from this stacking area, you can waste an awful lot of time driving across the site to reach it. Ismail wonders why they don't set up a second area on the opposite side of the site. He's sure it will save him 30 minutes a day. Multiply that by the number of forklift drivers and the construction company will be saving several hours per week that would be better spent ensuring supplies get to the various work-teams when they need them.
>
> Convinced that his idea is a good one, he suggests it to the site manager. Fortunately, the manager is committed to the idea of continuous improvement and decides to act on Ismail's suggestion.

What, would have happened if the manager wasn't committed to continuous improvement? The answer is possibly nothing at all – in which case, Ismail would probably never make a suggestion for change again. For continuous improvement to happen, management throughout an organization must be committed to achieving it and work at creating positive attitudes to change at all levels over a period of time. So all staff need to develop a proactive attitude to change. When it happens as part of an ongoing programme of improvement, they need to learn to welcome, rather than fear, it.

3 Tools for aiding continuous improvement

So far we've assumed that all you need to do in identifying areas for improvement in a process is to:

■ recognize where something is not going as well as it might;
■ think about what the causes are;
■ come up with ideas on how to tackle these causes.

Sometimes this is all you need to do. But in other situations you may need to undertake more careful analysis in order to discover the root cause of a problem. There are a number of tools you can use to help you do this. Here we are going to look at just three:

■ the five whys;
■ process flowcharting;
■ cause and effect diagrams.

3.1 The Five Whys

The Five Whys is a simple technique, developed by the Japanese, which consists of asking the question 'Why?' in relation to a particular process, outcome or event.

Let's take a straightforward example. You come home late one evening and find a stain on the sitting room carpet. You ask your teenage son 'Why did this happen?' Your son replies: 'Because a drink got knocked over.' You ask, 'Why did the drink get knocked over'. He replies 'Because I was fooling around with a couple of friends.' 'Why,' you ask, 'were you fooling around?' 'Because,' he replies, 'we were a bit drunk.' 'And why were you drunk?' 'Because we'd had some vodka as well as a few beers.' 'So why did you drink so much?' 'Because we've just finished our exams and wanted to celebrate.'

If you apply this process to a situation where there's a problem at work, you'll be surprised at how much you can learn about the connections between outcomes and causes. It could take more than five 'Whys' to find out the root cause of something, but usually five is quite enough.

Activity 21

5 mins

Imagine you work for the same charity as Uma. You have written an article for the bi-monthly newsletter and have been told that, no matter how busy you are, you will have to check the proof version and get it back to the Publications Department by the next day. 'Why the rush?' you ask Uma. 'Because,' Uma replies, 'we are way behind schedule.'

Knowing what you do about the Publications Department, try continuing this conversation using the Five Whys technique.

_____

_____

_____

_____

_____

_____

_____

_____

_____

_____

_____

There are a number of ways this conversation could go, but they should all end up with the same root cause. Here is one of them:

- 'Why are you behind schedule?'
- 'Because Sam sent the last section of text to the designer one week later than he was supposed to.'
- 'Why did he do this?'
- 'Because the contributor sent it to Sam very late.'
- 'Why did the contributor send it late?'
- 'Because he didn't make it a priority to get his feature written on time.'
- 'Why didn't he make it a priority?'
- 'Because he doesn't realize how important it is to meet the deadline we set him.'

Once the conversation has reached this point, it's time to consider how to improve the situation.

Activity 22

S/NVQ
C5

This Activity may provide the basis of appropriate evidence for your S/NVQ portfolio. If you are intending to take this course of action, it might be better to write your answer on separate sheets of paper.

Go back to the process you made notes about in Activity 19. Select one aspect of the process that is a problem and see whether you can find out the root cause of the problem by using the Five Whys technique. You should end up with a list of a maximum of five questions beginning with 'Why?', plus their answers.

_____

_____

_____

_____

_____

_____

_____

_____

_____

_____

_____

_____

_____

_____

3.2 Process flowcharting

Flowcharts are another tool that can help you to analyse a process and identify areas for improvement or problems and their solutions.

In its most simple form, a flowchart is a list of steps in a process, each of
which leads to the next one. Let's return to the example of the production of
the bi-monthly charity newsletter. If all goes well, the main steps should be as
follows:

1   People invited to contribute text plus suggestions for pictures

2   Contributions arrive

3   Contributions edited and pictures taken/found

4   Edited contributions sent to designer

5   Designer returns first proofs

6   First proofs checked by editor and necessary cuts made

7   Corrections on first proofs implemented by designer and second proofs
    returned to Publications Dept

8   Second proofs sent to contributors for their approval

9   Second proofs returned to Publications Dept

9   Corrections on second proofs implemented by designer and third proofs
    returned to Publications Dept

10 Third proofs checked by editor and returned to designer

11 Any final corrections implemented by designer

12 Artwork sent on disc to printer

These steps can be presented in the form of a flowchart, as shown on
page 42.

Flowchart of the ideal
process for producing
the charity newsletter

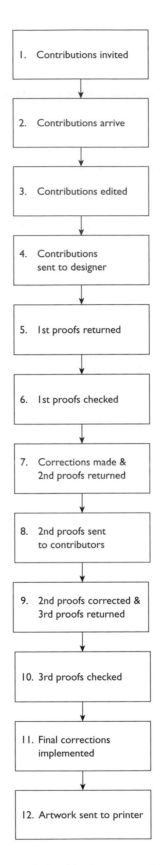

1. Contributions invited

2. Contributions arrive

3. Contributions edited

4. Contributions
   sent to designer

5. 1st proofs returned

6. 1st proofs checked

7. Corrections made &
   2nd proofs returned

8. 2nd proofs sent
   to contributors

9. 2nd proofs corrected &
   3rd proofs returned

10. 3rd proofs checked

11. Final corrections
    implemented

12. Artwork sent to printer

This, of course, is a picture of the ideal process. What happens in reality is rather different.

Activity 23

5 mins

Have a look at the flowchart and jot down some ways in which you think each step might go wrong.

_____

_____

_____

_____

_____

_____

You could produce a very long list of ways in which each step might go wrong. To name just some of them: for step 2, some contributions might arrive late, they might be badly written, too short or too long, have no suggestions for pictures, or be accompanied by low-quality photographs. For step 3 it might prove difficult to get hold of or take the requested pictures. For step 4 it might only be possible to send some of the text and pictures to the designer. For step 5 the proofs might be incomplete or late. And so on.

All the things that can go wrong can be graphically illustrated in a flowchart, like the one on page 44, which shows the process as it actually happens.

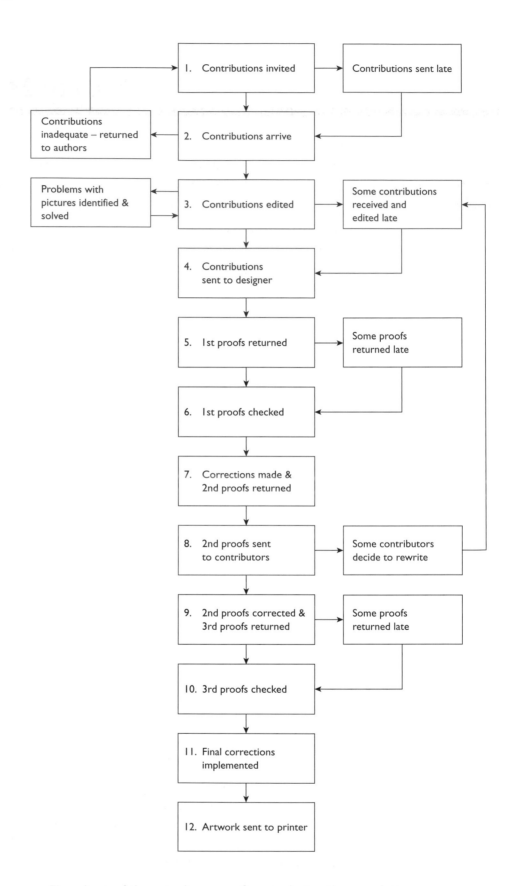

Flowchart of the actual process for producing the newsletter

Activity 24 · 20 mins

S/NVQ C5

This Activity may provide the basis of appropriate evidence for your S/NVQ portfolio. If you are intending to take this course of action, it might be better to write your answer on separate sheets of paper.

Return to Activity 19 and try drawing a flowchart of the process you chose in its ideal form. Then go through each step and list the various things that can go wrong. (You may want to try drawing a flowchart of the actual process, but this would take you more time than has been suggested for this Activity.)

At what steps in the process do you think changes could be made so that it is more likely to follow the ideal path? Note down a few ideas.

_____

_____

_____

_____

_____

_____

It's quite possible that doing this Activity will not have totally convinced you of the usefulness of flowcharting. It will at least partly depend on the complexity of the process you chose – if it only consists of a few steps you might well feel that you could manage perfectly well without it. However, you will find that when applied to a process made up of many steps in which there are lots of opportunities for things to go wrong, it can be very useful indeed.

3.3 Cause and effect diagrams

A cause and effect diagram is another tool for analysing processes. You will see its benefit as soon as you start to analyse processes in detail. Sometimes called a fishbone diagram because of its shape (or an 'Ishikawa' diagram after the person who devised it, Kaoru Ishikawa), it consists of a large arrow, into which smaller arrows lead. The large arrow represents a process or problem in a process. Each of the smaller arrows represents one of the main categories of inputs into the process, or possible causes of the problem. The categories will depend on the particular process you are looking at, but typical ones are:

- method (procedures);
- environment (physical conditions);

- personnel;
- equipment;
- materials;
- information or communication.

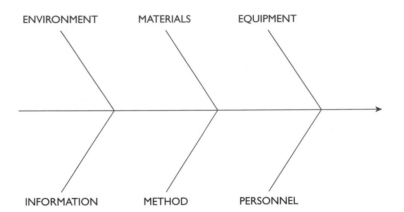

Typical categories in a cause and effect diagram

Activity 25  5 mins

Here are the beginnings of a cause and effect diagram for the process of producing the charity newsletter. What items would you add to each of the small arrows to make it more complete? Try to identify at least three and add them to the diagram.

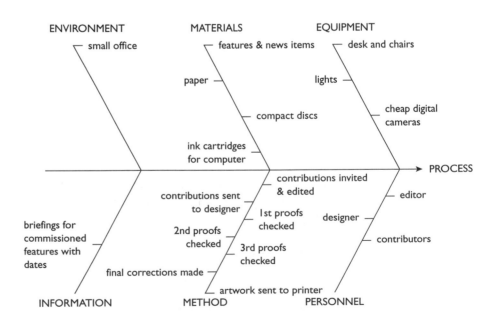

Among the most essential items missing from the diagram are the desks right next to each other (under environment); the Publications Officer (under personnel); a computer with modem (under equipment); an initial email calling for contributions (under information). You may well have thought of others.

If you take another look at the completed diagram, you can go through all the items and put a circle round anything you think presents an opportunity for improvement – as in the case of the features (their quality and late arrival) or the cheap digital camera.

You can see how this might be a useful tool for identifying possible improvements if you draw one that's relevant to your own situation.

Activity 26 · 15 mins

S/NVQ
C5

This Activity may provide the basis of appropriate evidence for your S/NVQ portfolio. If you are intending to take this course of action, it might be better to write your answers on separate sheets of paper.

Return one final time to the process you first identified in Activity 19 and try drawing a cause and effect diagram for it in the space below

Looking at the various items in your diagram, can you now add to the list of possible improvements that you drew up in Activity 4? Jot down any new ideas you have.

_____

_____

_____

4 The 5S Programme

As you will have gathered by now, if continuous improvement is to happen in an organization, everyone must get involved and take responsibility for it. One way of helping this process along is to introduce a 5S programme. Originating in Japan and first used in the UK by Japanese manufacturing companies – both on the shopfloor and in the office – it is now being adopted by other types of organization, such as construction companies.

The five 'S's are five Japanese words which few English speakers understand, so they are usually replaced with five English words beginning with S, such as:

- Sort
- Set in order
- Shine
- Standardize
- Sustain

Sometimes a sixth S – Safety – is added.

Some organizations prefer to use alternative versions of 5S, such as CANDO. This stands for:

- Cleanup
- Arranging
- Neatness
- Discipline
- Ongoing improvement

When you first look at these words you might think that 5S is all about good housekeeping. But it's actually a lot more than this, its aim being to create and maintain standardized and orderly operations.

4.1 The five steps of 5S

To get an idea of what each of the five steps entails, imagine a small, rather dingy metal-pressing factory. There are several large machines, all of which are dirty and covered with grease. On the floor, shoved into various corners, are boxes full of discarded materials. Various tools are strewn over the work-benches. In this situation, the staff often find it difficult to locate the tools they need. And when a machine breaks down it's often a big undertaking to find out where the problem lies. There's generally a feeling that things are a little chaotic and no one is surprised when the factory is late in getting an order out of the door.

In this situation, Step 1 of 5S, **Sort**, is about getting rid of everything that's not needed. The boxes of discarded materials can go for a start. Step 2, **Set in order**, means finding a place for everything that is needed. Where, for example, will all the tools go? Can workbenches be constructed where there is a clearly defined space for each one? Can more thought be given to the storage areas so that everyone knows exactly where to find stocks of particular materials and it's easy to spot when they are running out? Set in order also means ensuring that there is easy access to all areas and that the lighting is good.

Next comes Step 3, **Shine**, which is the job of making everything clean and tidy – and keeping it that way. When staff in the metal-pressing factory inspect the machines carefully they find all kinds of things that need to be taken care of, such as fittings caked with dirt, leaks of oil, and bolts loose or missing. There's also a fair amount of litter lying around the machines and workbenches that needs to be cleared away.

If the first three steps have been completed properly, everything should be ship-shape. But what next? How are the staff going to prevent the situation returning to what it was? Part of the answer is Step 4: **Standardize**. This means establishing and agreeing standards, and setting up systems for such things as the storing and handling of materials and getting rid of waste. It also means getting everyone into the habit of cleaning up throughout the day. (We will be returning to the subject of standards in the next section.)

Finally, there is Step 5: **Sustain**. This is about not only maintaining standards, but raising them. The key to doing this is to carry out a regular audit, at least once a week, of all physical aspects of the workplace, from walls, floors and walkways, to work benches, equipment and lighting. The audit is a fundamental part of any 5S programme, having a key role to play in the cycle of continuous improvement. It will reveal all the areas in which improvements could be made, ranging from small ones – such as the provision of more rubbish bins – to what might develop into major change projects, such as revising the layout of the factory.

Activity 27

Imagine you work in an office where a 5S programme is introduced. What kinds of things do you think might be done in each of the first three steps?

_____

_____

_____

_____

_____

_____

Most offices have unnecessary piles of paper – either scattered around on work surfaces or shoved into filing cabinets – all of which need to be sorted out and the unnecessary items discarded. The same can be said for computer desktops. There's also often a need to set everything in order by getting proper filing systems established – both for paperwork and for computer files. How many people have had the experience of not being able to find the document they need at a particular moment? Dirt may not be as much of a problem in offices as it is in some factories, but untidiness often is. 'Shining' is all about such things as not leaving piles of paper clips or rubber bands lying around, regularly clearing away the empty tea or coffee cups, and generally keeping the desktop free of unnecessary papers. Having a tidy, orderly office environment helps many people to think more clearly and work in a methodical way.

Activity 28 · 8 mins

Consider your own working environment. Jot down any ideas you have about the things that need to be done to:

- Sort it out
- Set things in order
- Make it 'shine'?

_____

_____

_____

_____

_____

_____

4.2 Visual management

You can help yourself and other people to maintain an orderly workplace – whether it's an office, factory, construction site or almost any other type of working environment – by using what is known as visual management. This involves using visually stimulating items, such as signs, lights, notice boards, and brightly or contrasting painted equipment, to catch people's attention and communicate important information.

The general rule is: 'The simpler, the better.'

In a factory or workshop setting, one simple example of visual management is the use of a shadow board. This is a board on which the shapes of various tools are painted, so that you only need to glance at it to see which tools are not in their allotted places. A similar device in an office is a piece of coloured tape run diagonally across the spines of a number of binders containing documents. Again, you only have to glance at the binders on the shelf to see a break in the line when a binder is not where it should be.

Another simple visual signal that is used in factory 5S programmes is the red tag. Suppose that someone carrying out an audit notices that equipment, materials or components have been left lying around, or that an item is dirty, defective or missing. The easiest way to alert people to the fact that there is a problem is to attach a red tag to the offending item, or the place where the item should be. The tag then stays there until corrective action has been taken.

Activity 29

5 mins

Notice boards can be an excellent way of passing on information and letting people know about what progress is being made in a 5S or any other type of programme. In fact, notice boards are among the items included in 5S audits. Some typical questions about them are listed overleaf. Try answering them in relation to your own workplace, making suggestions for improvements in the Comments column.

Noticeboards: key points	Yes	No	Comment
Are they positioned so that everyone has easy access to at least one?			
Is the display free of clutter and easy to read?			
Are the items on the boards relevant and up-to-date?			
Are the items well-designed, with easy-to-read text and eye-catching pictures?			
Other			

Visual management will help you to maintain a working environment that is orderly – and so more productive – on a continuous basis. So, too, will the setting of standards. In fact, setting standards is one of the keys to continuous improvement.

5 Standards and continuous improvement

Think of your last visit to the dentist. Did you have to wait long to check in at reception – and was the receptionist who checked you in friendly or off-hand? Did you have to sit in a waiting room that had several comfortable chairs, was well-lit, had a variety of recent magazines for you to read, and even had a few toys for small children to play with? Or did you have to wait in a small, dingy room with uncomfortable chairs and a pile of ancient magazines? Were you told that the dentist was ready to see you almost immediately, or did you have to wait an awfully long time as the sound of drilling came down the corridor?

Then, when you actually got into the dentist's room, did you feel it was a pleasant space in which you could feel reasonably relaxed – or exactly the opposite? Did you find your dentist pleasant, and the check-up and treatment relatively painless? Or did you dislike everything to do with the experience, from the way the dentist spoke to you to the way he or she dealt with your teeth?

And what about the actual treatment? Was the filling, for example, satisfactory, or did it feel a bit rough, with part of it breaking off a couple of months after it was done? Did the price of the treatment strike you as incredibly high or perfectly reasonable?

These questions have asked you about three different aspects of the service. These are:

- the structure – that is, the physical and organizational framework within which the service was given, such as the waiting room, the dentist's room, and the arrangements for checking in;
- the process – that is, the way you were treated on a personal level by the various members of staff, and the procedures followed by the dentist and his or her assistant in deciding what, if any, treatment you needed, and then delivering the treatment;
- the outcome – that is, the effect of the treatment plus its costs.

Any dentist who wants a flourishing practice will aim to provide a quality service – and this will mean drawing up standards for all three aspects. However, if the practice is to continue to flourish in the future, this will not be enough. The service will need to improve on a continuous basis, which means that once a standard has been met, a new standard will have to be drawn up.

All deliveries of materials to be unpacked and put in the correct place as quickly as possible.

How would you know when the standard had been met? The term 'as quickly as possible' can mean different things to different people and so cannot serve the function of giving everyone in the Stores Department a definite goal to achieve.

As well as being unambiguous, standards should also be realistic and achievable. It's no good setting standards that people have no chance of achieving with the available resources. The manager of the Stores Department, for example, should not set the standard 'All deliveries of materials to be unpacked and put in the correct place within 45 minutes of arrival on site' if he does not have enough staff to make this possible. If it's inevitable that staff will inevitably fail to meet a standard, they will end up being demotivated.

This brings us to another point about setting standards. It will not be easy to get staff to feel motivated about changing their working practices to meet a standard if they have not been involved in setting it. You should always consult with your team when drawing up standards.

Activity 30 · 10 mins

S/NVQ C5

This Activity may provide the basis of appropriate evidence for your S/NVQ portfolio. If you are intending to take this course of action, it might be better to write your answer on separate sheets of paper.

Pick out one area of work for which you are responsible and try writing a standard, if possible with another member of staff, that:

> You will need your answer to this Activity for Activity 31.

- represents an improvement in a work process or its outcome;
- is unambiguous;
- is achievable within the available resources.

5.1 Monitoring standards

As you've already seen, if standards are to form part of the cycle of continuous improvement, they must be monitored to discover whether they are being met. If they are not, then you will need to consider why, and plan how to ensure they are met in the future.

Use of audits

Exactly what method you use to monitor a standard will depend on what type of standard it is. Standards concerned with 'structure' – that is, the physical and organizational framework within which people work – can be monitored through auditing, as in a 5S programme. Take, for example, the standard:

All tools to be returned to their correct positions when not in use.

It's easy to see how you could include a relevant question on an audit form, to which the answer is Yes or No. You might even be able to assess the extent to which the standard is being met on a scale of 1 to 5 and make a comment on what more needs to be done.

AUDIT FORM

1 Tools and equipment	Yes	No	Extent of non-compliance/ compliance on scale of 1–5	Comment
Are all tools in correct positions when not in use?				

Other methods

Standards for processes and outcomes in manufacturing, where there is something tangible to be recorded – such as the number of defects in a week – are comparatively straightforward to monitor. The relevant data is collected and recorded in graphs which immediately show where there are problems.

Standards relating to the way a service is delivered are more difficult. Take the standard:

All customers should be made to feel welcome.

There is nothing that can be measured and recorded in a graph. One alternative is to ask customers for their views on whether the standard is being achieved, and then record their views in a table like the one below.

	Achieved	Partially achieved	Not achieved	What needs to be done
All customers made to feel welcome				

How the relevant information is gathered will depend on your particular situation. You can ask staff, customers, or both, to complete forms and questionnaires. You can ask staff to generally monitor their own performance, but also carry out some spot checks yourself. And in an organization committed to achieving quality, you can establish a quality circle and get them to monitor standards.

Activity 31

S/NVQ C5

Have a look at the standard you wrote for Activity 15. What method could you use for monitoring this standard and gathering the necessary information?

_____

_____

_____

_____

Monitoring standards will inevitably indicate areas where improvements can be made. Remember: standards are key to achieving change on a continuous basis.

6 Promoting continuous improvement

You've seen that a readiness to initiate change is at the heart of any attempt to increase quality on a continuous basis. But how do you get people to take the first step in initiating change – and start making suggestions for improvements – if they have never done this before? Two frequently used methods are:

- suggestion schemes;
- quality circles.

6.1 Suggestion schemes

Suggestion schemes can be aimed at individuals or teams. Some companies, particularly Japanese companies, have made their suggestion schemes reward-based. Toyota, for example, treats all suggestions as valuable, and pays for them even if some result in the company making a loss. This is because it accepts that the top 2.5% of suggestions more than counter-balance the losses.

Your organization may not want to do the same, but if you receive suggestions, bear in mind two aspects of the Toyota approach. Whenever Toyota receives suggestions, they are:

■ acknowledged within 24 hours;
■ evaluated within one week.

Activity 32

Why do you think it is important to acknowledge ideas within 24 hours and evaluate them within one week?

_____

_____

_____

You probably know from your experience that it is very discouraging to come up with an idea, only to feel that it has disappeared into a black hole. If staff are to keep on making suggestions for improvements, they need to feel that their ideas are appreciated and taken seriously. If they have to wait too long for any considered response to their ideas, they are likely to lose interest.

6.2 Quality circles

A quality circle involves regular meetings of a small group of volunteers who agree to:

■ identify, analyse and propose solutions to problems;
■ monitor the implementation of the planned solutions;
■ present their findings to management.

To succeed, a quality circle must be supported by managers and its leaders must be given training in skills such as facilitating. In practice, a quality circle often makes a big impact initially as people voice all the ideas they've been having for months – perhaps years – and management listens carefully. Then, as more quality circles are established throughout the organization, managers find they cannot cope with going to all the meetings they are expected to attend. Without the support of management, people begin to lose interest and stop coming up with ideas.

As a first line manager, you can play a major role in facilitating a quality circle, though you will certainly need the ongoing support of your manager if the circle is to be successful.

Some ways of helping people to come up with ideas for improvements are:

- suggesting ideas yourself;
- using techniques like brainstorming to get ideas going;
- encouraging the group to 'build' people's ideas.

Brainstorming

Brainstorming is a skill that needs to be learned by both a group and its leader. It can be extremely effective if carried out well but have disappointing results if not conducted correctly.

In brainstorming you ask members of the group to give you whatever ideas come into their head relating to a particular problem or situation. As they voice their ideas:

- you write exactly what they say on a flipchart;
- you don't stop to discuss or evaluate any of the ideas.

Only when the brainstorm is complete do you start to discuss and evaluate ideas and draw up a shortlist of the ones that are most feasible.

Building ideas

So how do you decide which ideas are the most feasible? It isn't very helpful to go through the list and promptly discard those that, on the face of it, don't seem useful. A better course of action is to try and build the ideas before you judge them. Ask the following questions.

- What's good about this idea?
- How can it be improved?
- Are there any ideas which might be combined with it?

Remember, the golden rule is not to judge or criticize an initial idea. Instead, focus on how it can be made to work.

Activity 33

10 mins

Here is an example of how brainstorming and idea building can together lead to an improvement in a process.

Tamsin worked as Office Manager of a small company supplying stationery to businesses. The company offices were spread over three floors in which there was just one high-quality photocopying machine. Numerous problems were associated with this arrangement. For a start, the machine was not easy to use and some people always struggled to work out which buttons to press and exactly which way round to put their paper. The same people also had difficulties with reloading the machine with paper and didn't know what to do when the light came on indicating that the toner was running low. Furthermore, the machine frequently broke down. Then, when it was working there was often a queue of people wanting to use it. It was particularly annoying to go to the machine to make a single copy, only to find that someone was in the middle of doing a bulk job.

All this caused a lot of unnecessary annoyance and conflict, so Tamsin decided it was time she and her team looked into the photocopying situation. At a meeting she wrote up the full list of problems and then led the team in a brainstorm for ideas on how to solve them. Among the ideas they came up with were:

- get rid of the big photocopier;
- put a small photocopier on every floor;
- appoint someone to make sure the photocopier is loaded with paper at the beginning of the day;
- put someone in charge of making sure that the toner is not about to run out;
- send bulk photocopying to a photocopier shop;
- appoint people to deal with problems like jammed paper;
- organize training for all staff on how to use the machine.

None of these ideas would provide the whole solution on their own, but combined and developed they could provide the company with the photocopying service it needs.

If you were Tamsin, how would you suggest combining and developing the various ideas that came out of the brainstorming session?

_____

_____

_____

_____

_____

_____

_____

_____

_____

Getting rid of the present big photocopier seems like a good idea – it breaks down far too often. However, a photocopier with the full range of facilities for enlarging, reducing, doing double-sided copies, and so on might be very necessary for the business. Perhaps the next step is to do some research on alternative photocopiers and their maintenance agreements. It is also a good idea to put a small photocopier on every floor. This will reduce the time people waste walking between floors to the photocopier and standing in queues. A possible next step is to decide how many copies people should be able to do on the small photocopiers, and in what situations they should use the large photocopier. Appointing someone, possibly on each floor, to take responsibility for filling up the copier with paper each morning, keeping an eye on the toner, and generally being on call to deal with problems might be a good idea. But this could become an onerous duty. It might be better to give a number of staff some proper training in how to operate the copiers and draw up a monthly rota for taking responsibility for the machine on your floor. Finally, whether it's a good idea to send bulk photocopying to a photocopier shop depends partly on whether this makes sense financially. Someone needs to conduct a cost–benefit analysis that takes into account how much staff time will be saved for other tasks by not having to do bulk photocopying in the office. (You can find what's involved in doing a cost–benefit analysis in the workbook in this series entitled *Managing Projects*.)

6.3 Communication

We have already seen that it is pointless to set up suggestion schemes and quality circles unless all levels of management are committed to creating a quality culture with a focus on continuous improvement. If this management commitment exists, one of the essentials for creating and maintaining commitment among staff is good communication. Your team will need to know:

- what the quality programme and continuous improvement entail;
- the targets or standards they should aim to meet;
- their roles and responsibilities;
- the training and support they will receive.

Activity 34

What methods might be used to communicate everything staff need to know about a quality programme and maintain their commitment:

- by your organization?
- by you within your team?

_____

_____

_____

The organization as a whole might use circulars, regular emails, posters, newsletters, meetings, seminars and study days. Within your team you need to hold formal regular meetings to keep people informed and discuss possible improvements in processes, products and services. You also need to make sure you have frequent one-to-one conversations with individual members. These conversations should provide an opportunity for staff to express their views and experiences about changes initiated through a programme of continuous improvement.

In this session we have focused on what's involved in getting people committed to the idea of continuous improvement. How to build on this commitment, to ensure that processes, products and services really are improved on a continuous basis, is the subject of another book in this series entitled _Implementing Change_.

Self-assessment 2

20 mins

For questions 1 to 5 complete the sentences with a suitable word or words from the following list:

CONDITIONS	PROCESSES	CAUSE
NEEDS	RESOURCES	FISHBONE DIAGRAM
PROCEDURES	FLOWCHART	STEPS

1 At the heart of continuous improvement is the idea that if customers' constantly changing _____ and wants are to be met, improvements must be made to _____ – and consequently products and services – in small _____, at all levels, forever.

2 You and your staff may have ideas for improvements regarding the physical _____ in which you work, the _____ you work with, your relationships with other people within and outside the organization, and the _____ you and your staff follow.

3 A useful tool for mapping out the steps in a process is a _____.

4 A useful tool for mapping out all the inputs to a process is a _____.

5 'Five Whys' is a useful technique for getting to the root _____ of a particular outcome or effect.

6 Which of the following do the 5 Ss stand for?

a Sort, Streamline, Shine, Set in order and Sustain
b Sort, Set in order, Shine, Standardize and Sustain
c Sort, Streamline, Shine, Standardize and Sustain
d Sort, Set in order, Streamline, Standardize and Sustain

7 Which of the following statements about 5S are TRUE and which are FALSE?

a Sorting is about finding a place for everything. TRUE/FALSE
b Setting in order is about arranging everything in neat piles. TRUE/FALSE
c Standardizing is about establishing standards and setting up systems for such things as storing and handling materials and getting rid of waste. TRUE/FALSE
d Sustaining is all about maintaining standards. TRUE/FALSE

8   If a suggestion scheme is to be successful, there are two things you should aim to do in response to each suggestion. The first is to acknowledge it within 24 hours. What is the other?

_____

9   Which of the following forms of communication do you NOT need in order to maintain commitment among staff to continuous improvement?

    a Written information from managers to staff.

    b Regular meetings between managers and staff as a group.

    c Appraisal meetings with individual members of staff.

    d Informal one-to-one conversations between managers and staff.

Answers to these questions can be found on page 103.

7 Summary

- Continuous improvement means continuously improving processes – and consequently products and services – in order to meet and then exceed customers' expectations.

- The benefits of continuous improvement were first recognized in Japan, where it is referred to as *kaizen*.

- As a manager you have a vital role to play in identifying ways in which processes can be improved, and encouraging your staff to do so.

- Improvements may be to do with:
  - the physical conditions in which you and your staff work;
  - the resources you and your staff work with;
  - the relationships you have with other people, both within and outside the organization;
  - the procedures you and your staff follow.

- Tools and techniques for aiding continuous improvement include:
  - 'Five Whys';
  - process flowcharting;
  - fishbone or cause and effect diagrams;
  - 5S programmes;
  - visual management.

- The 5 Ss are five Japanese words. One English-language version of the 5 Ss is:
  - Sort;
  - Set in order;
  - Shine;
  - Standardize;
  - Sustain.

- Fundamental to all 5S programmes is the process of auditing the workplace.

- Essential to continuous improvement is the setting and monitoring of standards.

- Standards can relate to:
  - structure – that is, the physical and organizational framework within which a service is provided or a product manufactured;
  - process – that is, the procedures employed in providing the service or manufacturing the product, and the way in which they are employed;
  - outcome – that is, the quality of the actual product or the effect of the service.

- Two ways of encouraging people to come up with ideas for improvements are:
  - suggestion schemes;
  - quality circles.

- The techniques of brainstorming and building ideas are useful for encouraging people to come up with ideas for improvements within quality circles.

- Both formal and informal communication are essential for creating and maintaining of commitment to continuous improvement among staff.

Session C
Preparing for change

1 Introduction

Have you ever had the experience of being summoned into your manager's office to be told that there are going to be some changes – perhaps in the way the company is structured, or in the IT systems it uses, or even in the location of its offices? If so, what was your reaction? Did your heart sink at the prospect of more change and the upheaval involved? You wouldn't be unusual if you thought 'Oh no!' We all know that we live in a changing world, but this doesn't necessarily make it easier to cope with change when it comes – particularly when it's imposed by others.

It is much easier to cope with change when you and your team have been involved in initiating the change, especially if you have used the tools and techniques of continuous improvement that you learnt in Session B. However, not all change comes about like that. Nevertheless, all changes, whether imposed or initiated by you and your team, will involve changes to systems and procedures and will need to be planned effectively. This Session will explore your role in preparing for change, starting by looking at what it means for the systems and procedures your team use.

2 Understanding systems and procedures

What do we mean by a 'system'? A system is:

'an organized or complex whole; an assemblage or combination of things or parts forming a complex whole'.

In other words, a system is a collection of the parts that together make up something that has a purpose of some kind. This definition covers:

- physical and mechanical systems;
- biological systems;
- and human and social systems.

Activity 35

Can you think of any example of:

- physical and mechanical systems;

_____

_____

- biological systems;

_____

_____

- and human and social systems.

_____

_____

The world is full of physical and mechanical systems. The house you live in, the car you drive, the food mixer in your kitchen, the computer in your office. It is also full of biological systems. People are biological systems, as are animals, plants, trees and every other living thing. What's more, people are parts of human and social systems, such as families, societies and communities, and organizations like companies, local councils, hospitals and schools or charities.

Despite all their differences, systems have somethings in common. They all take inputs from the world around them, transform them in some way into outputs back to the environment in which they live. Cars take in petrol or diesel and produce movement and exhaust fumes. Trees absorb carbon dioxide from the air and nutrients from the soil and their output is oxygen. Organizations take in energy, components and information, and their output consists of the products and services they supply.

All these systems can be illustrated by a general systems model like this:

Inputs   ⟶ | Transformation | ⟶ Output

Technically this is called an open system, because it interacts with its external environment – it takes things in and exports things to the environment. Nearly all social systems are open systems – those that aren't are completely closed off from the world. What's more, systems interact with other systems. The inputs to your system come from other systems and are passed on to other systems. You can divide one large system up into smaller sub-systems and see how they relate to each other.

In humans, the blood that keeps us alive is part of a system in which the heart pumps blood round the body and through the lungs to oxygenate it. But the lungs are part of a system that breathes in air and breathes out carbon dioxide. If your lungs don't function effectively, the blood can't be oxygenated properly and all the other sub-systems that rely on the blood supply won't work as well as they should.

Organizations are just like this. Problems in one part tend to affect others, and improvements in one sub-system will have knock on effects. By thinking of the organization as a system made of smaller sub-systems you will see just how inter-connected the various parts are.

Activity 36

10 mins

What does your organization take in from the environment and what is its output? What other systems does it interact with?

_____

_____

Any system can be described by answering five simple questions:

■ WHAT is the system for?	*What are its objectives, what is the intended outcome?*
■ WHO is involved in operating the system?	*The staffing of the operation, and also the physical resources employed.*
■ HOW are the resources employed to enable the system to operate?	*What do people and machines actually do? What are the work practices, roles and procedures?*
■ WHEN will the system function?	*The timescales employed, both start and finish times for individual sequences and the overall length of the operating cycle.*
■ WHERE will the system function?	*Locations for the various system operations and how much space they use.*

For example, two chicken farms produce chickens for people to eat, but their systems can be quite different:

	Farm 1	Farm 2
WHAT?	Producing chickens ready for slaughter at the lowest possible cost	Producing free range, organic chickens
WHO?	The farm manager and two technicians	A couple and their 27-year-old son
HOW?	In four large buildings using automated feeding systems	On 12 acres of a 350-acre mixed farm, with 40 mobile houses to move around the fields used
WHEN?	20,000, 10-week-old chickens, five times a year	5,000 chickens at roughly six monthly intervals
WHERE?	On the edge of a small town on part of a former farm	In a farm set amongst other farms in Somerset

Activity 37

10 mins

Use these five questions to describe your organization as a system.

WHAT?	
WHO?	
HOW?	
WHEN?	
WHERE?	

The third of these questions (How?) is the question about your organization's procedures. Procedures are the way that an organization works:

- the **rules** it operates by;
- the **roles** people perform;
- the physical **resources** people use, such as machines, equipment and vehicles and the buildings, facilities and physical environment in which they work; and
- the **routines** they follow – the way that they do their work.

Activity 38

20 mins

What are the main procedures that your team follows? What rules, roles, resources and routines define how they perform their tasks?

_____

_____

_____

_____

Why is it important to understand about systems and procedures when planning change? Because defining systems and procedures helps to make change possible. You can see what the organization looks like more clearly if you think of it as a set of systems and sub-systems that interact with each other, and see each system as containing a series of procedures made up of rules, roles, resources and routines. Before you can change what your team does, you need to know what it does. By thinking of your organization as a system and the tasks performed as part of that system as procedures, you are able to identify them more clearly and consider what the change involves.

Some organizations spell out the procedures in manuals or guidelines that define what people should do. These are very common when it comes to critical areas, such as health and safety or recruitment, but can also be valuable when dealing with the main operational procedures. However, procedure manuals are less use in customer service and professional activities, where the quality of the service is down to the personal interactions between people. When a customer service agent is working from a manual it usually means that customers are less satisfied than when they are working from detailed product knowledge and high level customer service skills!

3 The human and financial implications of change

People often define themselves by their job. Ask someone what they do and they will tell you their job, not their hobbies, games or other interest, or how they live their lives. Since we tend to describe ourselves by our jobs, it also means that our jobs are how we see ourselves as being. Change means that we are not just being asked to do something differently, but to change our perception of who we are. This is why people tend to resist change. The threat of change is not just that it might mean our jobs are at risk, but how we see ourselves as being is also at risk.

Highly skilled people see their skills being devalued if they are asked to do jobs differently, or train others to do them. Managers who define their status by the number of people they manage see themselves being demoted if they have a smaller team to lead, or promoted if their team gets bigger. Any change affects people in this way and means that you have to overcome significant barriers to change. There is more about this in the workbook *Implementing Change*.

Change also has financial implications. Most changes are introduced to increase revenue or income, or to stop potential or actual reductions. But the change itself will cost money which also has to be accounted for.

Activity 39 · 20 mins

What are the main costs of change going to be? Think of a change that you have experienced and see if you can identify the costs associated with it.

_____

_____

_____

_____

The costs of any change will vary according to the type of change and the scale. It is easy to identify the most obvious costs, such as having to invest in new capital (buildings, machines and equipment, software and vehicles) or in people (recruiting new people, making people redundant and training people). However, some of the costs may not be so obvious, such as the lost output if activities have to be suspended, higher waste or reject rates or reduced efficiency as people learn to work in different ways.

3.1 Cost–benefit analysis

One technique that can help to assess the potential costs and benefits is a cost–benefit analysis (CBA). Crudely, this adds up all the costs associated with the change and all the benefits. The costs are deducted from the benefits and the resulting figure shows the value of the change (if it's positive; if it's negative it raises questions as to why you are doing it.) We've already seen what the costs can be, but what about the benefits?

Activity 40

20 mins

What are the main benefits of change going to be? Think of a change that you have experienced and see if you can identify the benefits associated with it.

_____

_____

_____

One problem is putting a financial value on the benefits. A reduction in staff turnover may be beneficial for you, or an increase in quality may make your customers more satisfied, but will they add value to the organization? In general, the answer is yes, but quantifying it is often difficult.

Reduced staff turnover

It generally costs about 25% of a year's salary to replace someone. If you can cut staff turnover from three to two per year, by improving working conditions, then the value can be calculated on the basis that they are paid £16,000 pa, generating £12,000 savings over three years. Add to this that new employees tend to work at only ¾ efficiency during the first four months (because of training time, etc.), so one less new recruit per year over three years adds a further £3,000 saving (¼ of four months' salary – £4k – for three years). So if the cost is less than £15,000, then the change pays for itself.

Increase in quality

The starting point for quality improvements is reduced returns, complaints or customer churn. A returned item that has to be refunded or replaced has a clear values. Complaints are less easy to cost. They may lead to refunds or replacements, but they also take up people's time and cause customers to warn off others from using you. Customer churn (the rate at which new customers have to be found to replace lost customers) is something that many larger organizations are very aware of, but smaller ones are less aware. Imagine that your organization has 2,000 customers every year. 1,500 are repeat customers and 500 have been recruited to replace lost customers. It has a 25% churn rate, as 25% of all customers have to be replaced. To grow the business your organization needs to recruit more than 500 customers every year. If it spends £40,000 on recruiting new customers then those 500 new customers cost £80 each. An improvement in the quality of your products or services, or in customer service, may reduce the churn rate to 20% (400 customers), a saving of £8,000 per year.

It's important to stress that the quality savings are not necessarily going to be felt by reduced expenditure but by existing expenditure being more effective as the 500 new customers recruited will grow the business by 100 new customers, each of whom will contribute to growth in total revenue. This works fine in the private sector but can be problematic in the public sector, where extra customers don't necessarily produce extra revenue. In 2006, many hospitals and other NHS organizations found themselves in financial trouble because improved quality of service (such as faster treatment times) had increased costs but not revenues. This is why CBA is so important. Before making any changes look at the financial costs and benefits and use this in your planning of the change.

3.2 Breakeven analysis

A technique associated with CBA is breakeven analysis. Essentially, this takes account of the time period over which costs and benefits occur. Generally the costs of change are incurred upfront, and the benefits accrue over time. Breakeven occurs when the financial benefits have added up to cover the costs, if they do. Unfortunately, the costs and potential benefits are calculated upfront but then, too often, are not monitored because nobody wants to admit that the benefits have not been as great as they were projected to be, or something else happened making them hard to quantify. Organizations that don't measure the effects of change will never learn from their experience. If a change project was thought to be worth doing then it's worth seeing if it worked as expected. If there is no attempt to measure the actual costs and benefits then why bother to make any financial case in advance?

One of the problems with change is that the costs of change are very hard to recoup. They are what is known as sunk costs. The money has been spent but can't be recovered, other than through the second-hand value of some machinery or equipment. Training in skills that aren't used, or time spent planning and costing a project have all been paid for and there's no way that the money can be returned. If it's expected that the benefits will outweigh the costs in three years' time, but by then the market has changed, the change itself has been changed, and the person who led it has moved on and nobody 'owns' the change. Whilst there are good reasons not to monitor and review change projects if it is no longer possible, this should be the exception rather than the rule. Good management of change is based on learning from experience, and that can only be done if you know what happened, and why.

If you want to learn more about CBA and breakeven analysis, they are covered in detail in the workbook *Managing Projects*.

4 Planning the project activities

Once you have established the aims and objectives of the change project you need to set about planning exactly how you are going to achieve them – that is, establishing the key project activities and the order in which they should be completed. If you have not been able to do so before, this is certainly the point at which you need to involve your team.

There are a number of tools you and your team may find very useful in planning the project activities. The main ones are:

- logic diagrams;
- critical path diagrams;
- Gantt charts.

NB: These topics are also covered in *Implementing Change*.

4.1 Logic diagrams

Constructing a logic diagram will help you to identify the key stages in the project and the order in which they should occur. Begin by establishing with your team what the main activities in the project will be: first write everyone's ideas on a whiteboard or flipchart and then decide what the main activities actually are. You don't want to end up with an unmanageable number. You can then write each activity on a sticky-note or piece of adhesive coloured card and arrange these on the flipchart or board until you have them in a logical order. The final step is to draw the diagram with arrows between the stages.

Stella is the manager of a health club. She has been talking to clients and discovered that they wanted more yoga classes, and also to have the chance to do classes in the Alexander technique and in Pilates.

The clients also had a lot to say about how the gym was run. For a start, they didn't like the way there were bottlenecks for some pieces of equipment during peak times. But more fundamental was the feeling that no one on the staff took a personal interest in them once their initial exercise regime had been established at the beginning of the year.

Finally, there was the café. Not only did they want the décor to be improved, they also wanted a better selection of drinks and snacks.

Stella produced a proposal taking all the new data into account and she secured the go-ahead from the owner. During discussions of the proposal with the staff, it was decided that the main activities were as follows:

A   Draw up detailed proposals for redesign of reception area and café.

B   Consult with clients on their views about designs and amend accordingly.

C   Organize redecoration and installation of new furniture.

D   Consult with clients on drinks and snacks they want in café.

E   Organize deliveries of requested drinks and snacks.

F   Establish procedures for checking state of changing and shower facilities, and cleaning during day.

G   Draw up rota for checking and cleaning procedures.

H   Establish procedures for checking equipment in gym every day and arranging for any broken equipment to be repaired.

I   Draw up rota for checking equipment.

J   Draw up new list of classes.

K   Consult with clients on list of classes to establish best times plus level of demand.

L   Recruit teachers for classes.

M   Organize and run client care session for teachers to stress importance of turning up on time and being well-prepared.

N   Set up appointments system for gym during peak periods (lunchtimes and evenings).

O   Organize client care session for all non-teaching staff, with emphasis on how to look after clients in gym.

P   Run client care sessions.

Q   Establish system for ensuring that clients in gym receive personal attention from one staff member throughout the year.

R   Organize publicity brochure.

S   Distribute publicity brochure.

Activity 41

3 mins

In the list above:

■ Which activities could be combined?

_____

■ Which activities should, ideally, be carried out first, in parallel with each other?

_____

Activities B, D and K, all of which involve consulting with clients, could be carried out at the same time. So too, perhaps, could Activities M and O, both of which are concerned with giving staff training in client care.

Activities A, F, H, J, and N should all, ideally, be carried out first in parallel with each other. (R – Organize publicity brochure – is another possibility, but it's probably best to produce this after the consultation exercise has been completed.) Whether this is actually possible in practice will depend on the number of staff available. It would be no good getting so many staff involved in the change project at any one time that they couldn't continue with the day-to-day work of running the club at least to present standards.

In fact, Stella and her team decided that they could carry out A, F, H, J and N in parallel, and so ended up with the logic diagram on the next page.

There are a number of things to notice about this diagram:

■ The diagram begins with 'Start' and ends with 'Finish'.
■ The arrows show which activities are dependent on other activities.
■ There is no timescale.
■ No activities are assigned to people.

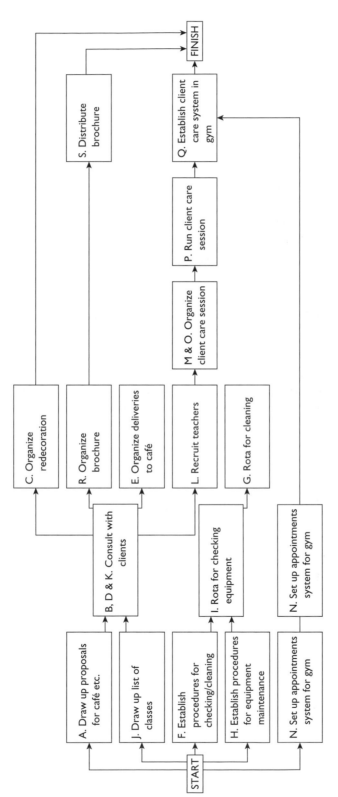

Logic diagram for health club change project

4.2 Critical path diagrams

A critical path diagram is a useful tool for estimating precisely the time a change project will take, and drawing up a schedule. A critical path diagram (also known as a network analysis) is a useful tool for doing this, as it shows how long individual activities should take and the relationship between them.

Let's first assume you haven't been given a completion date that you must achieve. The first step is to look at each of the main activities included in your logic diagram and decide with your team:

- what the activity consists of and how long it will take;
- which staff should carry it out:
- given the existing workload of those staff, how many days/weeks/months it will take them to complete the activity.

Taking all these factors into account, here is Stella's list of estimated times for activities:

Key activity		Estimated time in weeks
A	Draw up proposals for redesign of reception area and café	2
B, D, K	Consult with clients	3
C	Organize redecoration and installation of new furniture	4
E	Organize deliveries of requested drinks and snacks	1
F	Establish checking and cleaning procedures	1
G	Draw up rota for checking and cleaning procedures	1
H	Establish procedures for maintenance of gym equipment	1
I	Draw up rota for checking equipment	1
J	Draw up new list of classes	1
L	Recruit teachers for classes	8
M, O	Organize client care session	1
N	Set up appointments system for gym during peak periods	1
P	Run client care session	Half-day
Q	Establish system for client care in gym	2
R	Organize and produce publicity brochure	6
S	Distribute brochure	2

If you now add times to the various activities in the logic diagram, you will see which route from Start to Finish will take the **longest** time. This route is the critical path – the **minimum** amount of time it will take to complete the project.

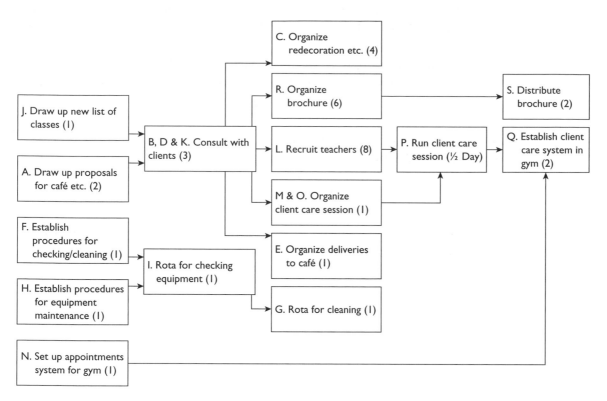

Critical path diagram for health club change project

In Stella's diagram, the critical path is A (two weeks), K (three weeks), L (eight weeks), P (half a day) and Q (two weeks) – a total of 15 weeks. So if everything goes according to plan, the whole project should take less than four months. In reality, there could be some slippage. It may, for example, take more than eight weeks to recruit all the teachers. However, the diagram does establish the basis for week-by-week planning and monitoring.

Activity 42

8 mins

You can practise producing your own logic and critical path diagrams by starting with something simple, such as preparing a meal. Imagine you are asked to prepare the following menu:

- scrubbed and boiled new potatoes;
- cheese omelette;
- salad with dressing;
- strawberries and cream.

Draw a logic diagram and then a critical path diagram with the time for each task in minutes.

The task that is going to take the longest time in this menu is scrubbing and boiling the new potatoes. In fact, it is probable that this task alone will constitute your critical path. Parallel to it will be all the other tasks. All you need to do is work out how long each one is going to take and the best order in which to do them, ending with cooking the omelette.

4.3 Gantt charts

A Gantt chart, which is often in the form of a bar chart, shows all the key activities and when they should begin or end. (The activities are listed down the left-hand side and the timescale appears across the top.) The chart doesn't, however, show the relationship between different activities as clearly as a critical path diagram.

A Gantt chart for Stella's project would look like the one on page 81.

In this chart, a number of activities are all shown starting in the first week. But in fact, if the main priority is to get all elements of the project completed by the time the publicity brochure is distributed, rather than making lots of small improvements over a period of time, there are a number of activities that could be completed as late as week 13 (Activities F, G, H, I and N). These activities have what is referred to as 'float'. This is shown on the chart by the addition of a line. It's also apparent that organizing the client care session for staff (Activity M) could begin earlier. This activity is therefore said to have 'slack'. It's always useful to have some activities with float or slack as they will give you some flexibility in the schedule, which will probably be much-needed.

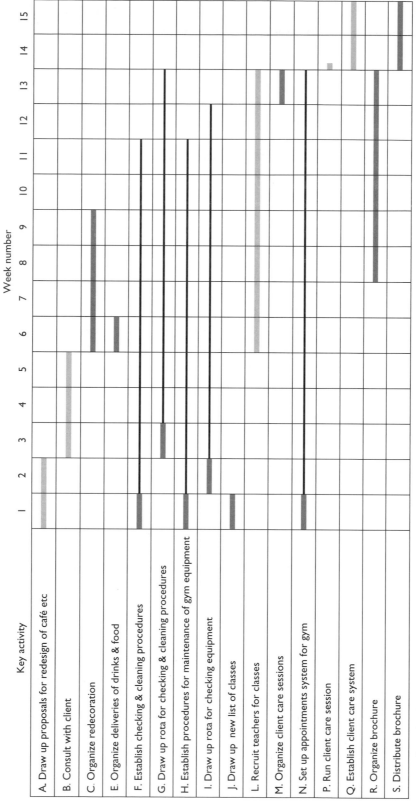

Gantt chart for health club change project

Key activity	Week number

Critical path activities ▮ Activities not on critical path ▮ ▬ Line indicating float time

Activities:
- A. Draw up proposals for redesign of café etc
- B. Consult with client
- C. Organize redecoration
- E. Organize deliveries of drinks & food
- F. Establish checking & cleaning procedures
- G. Draw up rota for checking & cleaning procedures
- H. Establish procedures for maintenance of gym equipment
- I. Draw up rota for checking equipment
- J. Draw up new list of classes
- L. Recruit teachers for classes
- M. Organize client care sessions
- N. Set up appointments system for gym
- P. Run client care session
- Q. Establish client care system
- R. Organize brochure
- S. Distribute brochure

Activity 43

The health club project has several sub-projects, one of which is to produce and distribute a publicity brochure. The critical path analysis for this sub-project looks like this:

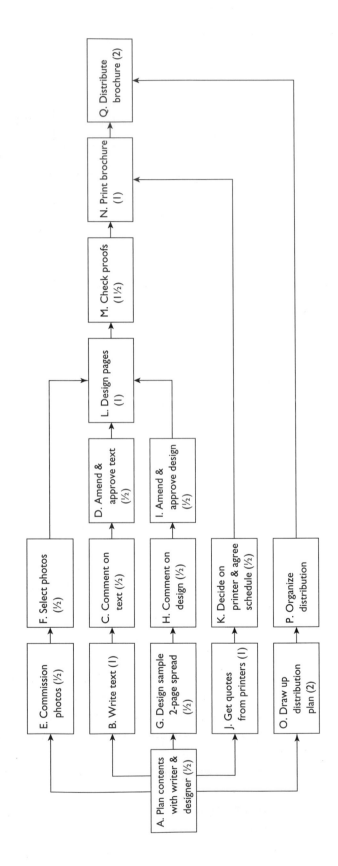

Try producing a Gantt chart for this sub-project using the outline overleaf.

Week number

Activity	1	2	3	4	5	6	7	8

Other information that can be added to a Gantt chart includes:

- milestones (that is, special points where you think it's important to check on progress so far), perhaps represented by a diamond or triangle
- project meetings, perhaps represented by a circle.

As you can see, it is a fairly easy task to draw a Gantt chart. However, computer software is available that will enable you to try out a number of different scenarios very quickly, showing what will happen if an activity takes a longer or shorter period of time than you originally forecast. Using the software will also make life much easier when it comes to monitoring the project's progress and making any necessary adjustments from week to week.

You can see a completed Gantt Chart on page 102.

When drawing up a project plan, you need to bear in mind that plans have a tendency to go astray. So always aim to build some contingency time into your plan – and possibly some contingency resources – to help you cope with the unexpected. There are all sorts of ways in which things could go wrong for Stella: a vital staff member could fall ill; there may be a delay in the delivery of the furniture; there may be a problem with getting a piece of equipment fixed, and so on. Rather than telling the club owner that the project will be completed in under four months, she should make it clear that this is the **minimum** amount of time it will take.

5 Establishing responsibilities and methods of communication

As well as sorting out the key project activities and overall schedule, you need to establish exactly who is responsible for what. Whether you do this during the stage of planning the activities, or afterwards, will depend on the particular situation. However, whenever you do it, remember that if your team is to feel empowered, every member must have an established responsibility within the project.

Going back to Stella and the health club, for example, she would be making a big mistake if she thought she could manage all the key activities herself. In one of the initial team meetings it needs to be agreed exactly who will take responsibility for organizing the customer survey, who will take responsibility for sorting out the refurbishment of the café and reception area, and so on. In this particular example, the ideal time to do this may have been after the team had drawn up the logic diagram but before they started on the critical path diagram. However, this may not always be the case.

5.1 Identifying possible effects

Giving people new responsibilities not only means empowering them; it also means identifying what new skills they need to acquire. If they require further training, this may have the knock-on effect of an additional cost.

You will also need to consider the effects of the change not only on each member of your team, but also on the people outside your team – that is, the 'ripple' effects. It's essential that you discuss your plans for change with these people and together make an assessment of how they will be affected. You may need to consider ways of amending your plan to accommodate the requirements of people outside your team. Going through this process will have the added benefit of helping to break down any existing barriers between departments.

One major question to consider is: who is likely to resist the change, and how will you deal with this resistance? Never ignore signs of resistance or try to overcome it just by repeating arguments in support of change. Instead, attempt to understand the reasons for the resistance and be prepared to discuss these while pointing to the possible benefits of change for the individuals concerned. (You will find more on resistance to change, and how to respond to it, in another workbook in the series entitled *Implementing Change*.)

Activity 44

15 mins

S/NVQ C5

This Activity may provide the basis of appropriate evidence for your S/NVQ portfolio. Whether or not you are intending to take this course of action, write your answers on separate sheets of paper.

Look back at your notes in Activities 19, 22, 24 and 26 on a change project and consider the following questions:

a　How will each individual in your team be affected by the change?

_____

_____

b　What further training or development activities, if any, do they need to take part in?

_____

_____

c　Which other groups (if any) will be affected? How will they be affected?

_____

_____

d　What role should you play in dealing with these effects?

_____

_____

e　What are the likely effects (if any) on costs of all of the above?

_____

_____

5.2 Identifying lines and methods of communication

If the project is to run smoothly, you also need to ensure that there is good communication throughout. This means not only two-way communication between you and your team, but also keeping people outside the project informed about progress.

Activity 45 · 8 mins

S/NVQ
C5

This Activity may provide the basis of appropriate evidence for your S/NVQ portfolio. Whether or not you are intending to take this course of action, write your answers on separate sheets of paper.

Look back at your notes in Activities 19, 22, 24 and 26 on a change project and consider the following questions:

a   Who are the people who need to be kept informed?

_____

_____

_____

b   At what stages in the project should they be informed?

_____

_____

_____

c   What are the best ways of informing them?

_____

_____

_____

The people who need to be kept informed will certainly include your manager. They may also include people in other departments or teams in your organization as well as all the members of your own team. The methods you use may include:

- memos and/or emails;
- regular written reports on progress, with reference to milestones;
- informal one-to-one conversations with your manager and team members;
- regular progress meetings with the whole team;
- ad hoc meetings with the team to sort out major problems as they arise.

It's a good idea to include team progress meetings in your schedule. However, never regard these as a substitute for other forms of communication. Rather, always be ready to listen and respond appropriately to the concerns voiced by members of your team and so keep up the team's morale.

We will return to the subject of communication in the next session.

Self-assessment 3

20 mins

1 Complete the systems diagram below.

2 What five question words help you to define a system?

- W_____?
- W_____?
- H_____?
- W_____?
- W_____?

3 What are the four Rs that describe the way that an organization works?

- R_____
- R_____
- R_____
- R_____

4 What two potential costs and two potential benefits could a change project bring for an organization?

Potential costs   Potential benefits

1.   1.

2.   2.

For questions 5 to 7, circle the type of diagram that is being described.

5 This is in the form of a bar chart which shows all the key activities and when they should begin or end.

   LOGIC DIAGRAM/CRITICAL PATH DIAGRAM/GANTT CHART

6 This helps you to identify the key stages in a project and the order in which they should occur.

   LOGIC DIAGRAM/CRITICAL PATH DIAGRAM/GANTT CHART

7 This shows the relationship between different activities, identifying which activities may run in parallel to each other and which must follow on consecutively from each other.

   LOGIC DIAGRAM/CRITICAL PATH DIAGRAM/GANTT CHART

8 In a Gantt chart some activities have 'slack', while others have 'float'. Which of the following statements about these terms are correct?

   a An activity is said to have 'float' if its completion date could be earlier than that shown in the chart. CORRECT/NOT CORRECT
   b Float is shown on the chart by the addition of a line. CORRECT/NOT CORRECT
   c An activity is said to have 'slack' if its completion date could be later than that shown in the chart. CORRECT/NOT CORRECT
   d Slack is shown on the chart by the addition of a line. CORRECT/NOT CORRECT

   Answers to these questions can be found on page 104.

6 Summary

■ Understanding systems and procedures can help you to design new ways of working.

■ Systems can be defined by asking the five questions What?, Who?, How?, Where? and When?

■ Procedures can be defined by the Rules, Roles, Resources and Routines being used.

■ The human and financial implications of change need to be considered, and the costs and benefits calculated.

■ Cost–benefit analysis and breakeven analysis provide the basis for reviewing and learning from any change project.

■ Tools to help you in planning how you are going to achieve a project's aims and objectives are:

  ■ logic diagrams;
  ■ critical path diagrams;
  ■ Gantt charts.

■ Constructing a logic diagram will help you to identify the key stages in a project and the order in which they should occur.

■ A critical path diagram shows the relationship between different activities, identifying which activities may run in parallel to each other and which must follow on consecutively from each other.

■ A Gantt chart is a bar chart that shows all the key activities in a project and when they should begin and end. Computer software is available that will not only help you to draw Gantt charts but also try out different scenarios very quickly.

■ Once the project activities have been planned, you need to establish responsibilities. You also need to ensure that there will be effective communication both within your team and with people outside it.

Performance checks

1 Quick quiz

Jot down the answers to the following questions on *Planning Change in the Workplace*.

Question 1   What are the six kinds of forces for change represented by the initials PESTLE?

_____

_____

Question 2   Give two examples of how environmental forces for change have affected organizations in the last 30 years or so.

_____

_____

_____

Question 3   What do the initials SWOT stand for?

_____

_____

Question 4   In the cycle of continuous improvement, you do something and then review what has been done. What are the next two steps?

_____

_____

_____

Question 5   What is the Japanese name for continuous improvement?

_____

Question 6   Most small improvements in the workplace can be placed in one of four categories. Two of these are: the physical conditions in which you work, and resources. What are the other two categories?

_____

Question 7   What does the Five Whys technique consist of?

_____

_____

_____

Question 8   Why is flowcharting a helpful tool in identifying areas for improvement in a process?

_____

_____

_____

Question 9   In a cause and effect, or fishbone, diagram, what does the main horizontal arrow usually represent?

_____

Question 10   In a cause and effect, or fishbone, diagram, the small arrows represent inputs. Categories of inputs vary, but often include method (procedures) and environment (physical conditions). Can you name two others?

_____

Question 11   If three of the 5 Ss are Sort, Set in order and Shine, what are the other two?

_____

Question 12   Red tagging is a form of visual management. What does it consist of?

_____

_____

_____

Question 13   How does the setting of standards play a vital part in any programme of continuous improvement?

_____

_____

_____

Question 14   What does a critical path diagram show about the key activities in a project? What does a Gantt chart show?

_____

_____

Answers to these questions can be found on page 106.

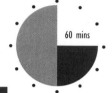

■ 2 Workbook assessment

Read the following example about someone identifying a possible improvement in a process which will affect other parts of the organization. Answer the questions below, writing your answers on a separate sheet of paper.

> Ben works as the manager of the unit assembly team in a factory producing electrical heaters. When a 5S programme is introduced, it quickly became apparent that the difficulties Ben's team face amount to rather more than old and grubby benches. The various parts that are to be assembled arrive from different parts of the factory in boxes that take up a lot of space and are often difficult to unpack. Furthermore, there is sometimes a shortage of one or more parts.
>
> When Ben starts to look into all this he realize that a basic cause of the problem is that the various assembly activities are scattered around the factory. As far as he can see, it makes much more sense for plastic casing assembly, switch assembly, motor and fan assembly, and heater coil assembly to be brought together in one place with unit assembly. He decides to arrange a meeting with his manager to discuss his idea for improvement and what he should do about it.

Imagine you are Ben's manager. What advice will you give him in this and subsequent meetings about:

■   what he should do before he even begins to consider drawing up a proposal for change;
■   what tasks he should undertake in drawing up a proposal for change;
■   whom he should discuss his ideas with and how he should go about winning their support for change.

Your complete answer to this assessment need not be longer than a single page.

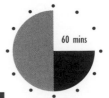

60 mins

3 Work-based assignment

S/NVQ
C5

The time for this assignment gives you an approximate idea of how long it is likely to take you to write up your findings. You will find you need to spend some additional time gathering information, perhaps talking to colleagues and thinking about the assignment.

This assignment may provide the basis of appropriate evidence for your S/NVQ portfolio.

What you have to do

For this assignment you are asked to identify and plan how to implement a significant change for your team that will bring about improvements in the way that they work. Start by using the outcomes of Activities 6, 8, 11, 12, 14, 15 and 16 to help you identify what changes are needed and why.

You should involve your team in agreeing the pressures for change and what changes are needed. You should also consult others who may be affected, especially your manager, and collect whatever data is needed to help you understand the factors that will influence its success or failure.

You should then involve your team in identifying how the change could be implemented, using any of the techniques that you have learnt about to help you. You should also consider what the present and possible future systems would be like, and identify any new procedures that would be needed.

You can also consider the implications of introducing the change, including assessing the costs and benefits and how these might be monitored to determine how successful the change turns out to be.

What you have to write

Write down your recommendations and your plan for bringing about the change as a proposal to your manager or other relevant person. The whole document does not have to be more than two or three pages long. Include this written recommendation plus any supporting evidence in your portfolio.

Reflect and review

▣ 1 Reflect and review

Now that you have completed your work on *Planning Change in the Workplace*, let's review our workbook objectives together.

The first workbook objective was as follows.

- You should be better able to identify the forces behind change and how they might affect your organization and team.

We reviewed six major forces behind changes of all kinds: political, economic, social, technological, legal and environmental factors. Political factors arise from the policies pursued by the government of the day, some of which may have an effect on economic factors. In fact, it's not always easy to decide whether a factor is political or economic. Of course, some economic factors have nothing to do with government policies, arising as they do out of events beyond the government's control.

Social factors may be long term – such as changes in the composition of the population – or fleeting, as in the case of fashion in clothes and food. The same can be said of technology, which drives change along at a relentless pace. New laws and regulations, some of them relating to environmental issues such as pollution and the need to preserve finite resources, also bring about change, as do environmental developments themselves and the public's response to them.

As a leader of change, it is useful for you to be able to identify which of these factors are in operation when a change occurs at work. It is even more valuable to make yourself aware of known developments so that you can identify possible threats or opportunities for your organization. Such threats and opportunities could lead to changes with possible effects on both you and your team.

You may want to ask yourself the following questions regarding these points.

■ To what extent do I spend time considering the causes of change in my work?

_____

_____

_____

■ How could I find out more about events which may result in changes in my organization, and so possibly in my job and the jobs of my team, in the future?

_____

_____

_____

The second workbook objective was as follows.

■ You should be better able to recognize the beneficial aspects of change, whether it be through continuous improvement or through one-off projects.

We have looked at both the 'up' and the 'down' sides of change. When change takes place as part of a programme of continuous improvement aimed at increasing quality, it can be initiated by any member of a team. It does not necessarily provoke the negative feelings people often have in response to change imposed by senior management. These negative feelings, along with any drawbacks of a proposed change, need to be recognized from the outset if they are not to present unexpected snags.

However, you and your team will stand to benefit most from a change if you are able to recognize and communicate its good points. These include:

■ bringing **new interest** to the job;
■ opening up new prospects for **career development**;
■ showing a **new slant on things**;
■ providing the opportunity to learn **new skills**;
■ posing a **challenge**;
■ giving an opportunity to **empower** the team.

You may feel the following questions are appropriate when considering the implications of a proposal.

■ How can I and my team members get the most from this change?

_____

_____

_____

■ In what ways can the change be used as a step towards new career developments for each of us?

_____

_____

_____

■ How can we meet the challenge of this change and find new interest in the work through it?

_____

_____

_____

■ What is good about this change?

_____

_____

_____

The third objective was:

■ You will be better able to initiate improvements in workplace activities.

There is always scope for improvement in any of the following:

■ the physical conditions in which you and your staff work;
■ the resources you and your staff work with;
■ the relationships you have with other people both within and outside the organization;
■ the procedures you and your staff follow.

If you make a point of always being on the look-out for possible improvements in any of these areas, you will be contributing to a process of continuous improvement – something that more and more organizations are considering essential to their continuing success and prosperity.

Of course, there is more to initiating improvements than just identifying where they are needed. Before taking any action you may have to investigate the root cause of a problem, using such tools as flowcharts, cause and effect diagrams and the Five Whys.

You may want to ask yourself the following questions regarding these points:

■ How can I ensure that I identify areas for improvement on a continual basis and actually do something about them?

_____

_____

_____

■ Do I feel confident about using the tools described in this workbook for identifying the root causes of problems? If not, how might I go about building up this confidence, and perhaps even learning about other tools associated with continuous improvement?

_____

_____

_____

The next objective was:

■ You should be better able to describe the effect of change on systems and procedures and assess the costs and benefits of change.

Unless you can appreciate how the different systems in your organization relate to each other and to those outside, you will not be able to bring about changes that fit easily into them. You also need to be able to specify the procedures, especially if they are critical, to ensure that the team is able to perform effectively in their new roles. But, as well as being able to describe the new systems and procedures, you should be able to make a financial case for them. This means identifying the costs and benefits that the change will bring, and be willing to monitor the effectiveness of the change in bringing about these benefits, something that is far more likely if the change has been planned and communicated effectively.

■ What systems and procedures are relevant to the work of my team, including the systems in other parts of the organization and outside it that we interact with?

_____

_____

_____

Could I clearly identify the costs and benefits of change in my organization? Who would be able to help me?

_____

_____

_____

The final workbook objective was:

■ You will be better able to plan change projects.

A huge amount of work can go into planning major change. In fact, in some cases it's better to think of a major change as a number of projects rather than one. Whatever the size of the project, there are always certain processes that you will need to go through, such as:

■ collecting information;
■ establishing the aims and objectives;
■ establishing the timescale and necessary resources (including budget and staff);
■ assessing the feasibility of the project;
■ identifying the necessary activities and planning the order in which they are to be done, and by whom.

There are various tools you can use in planning projects, such as critical path diagrams and Gantt charts. For larger projects you will find them indispensable.

Two questions you may like to ask yourself are:

■ To what extent have I properly planned change in the past? What are the main areas in which I have not been sufficiently thorough in my planning?

_____

_____

_____

■ How might I improve my project-planning skills, including the use of critical path diagrams and Gantt charts?

_____

_____

_____

2 Action plan

Use this plan to further develop for yourself a course of action you want to take. Make a note in the left-hand column of the issues or problems you want to tackle, and then decide what you want to do, and make a note in column 2.

The resources you need might include time, materials, information or money. You may need to negotiate for some of them, but others could be easy to acquire, like half an hour of somebody's time, or a chapter of a book. Put whatever you need in column 3. No plan means anything without a timescale, so put a realistic target completion date in column 4.

Finally, describe the outcome you want to achieve as a result of this plan, whether it is for your own benefit or advancement, or a more efficient way of doing things.

Desired outcomes				
1 Issues	2 Action	3 Resources	4 Target completion	
Actual outcomes				

3 Extensions

Extension I

Book	*Kaizen strategies for successful organisational change*
Author	Michael Colenso
Edition	2000
Publisher	FT Prentice Hall

This book provides good coverage of the relationship between kaizen and change management. It includes explanations of kaizen terms such as the 5 Ss, IIT, *gemba, poka-yoke*, and so on.

4 Answers to activities

Activity 43 on pages 82–3

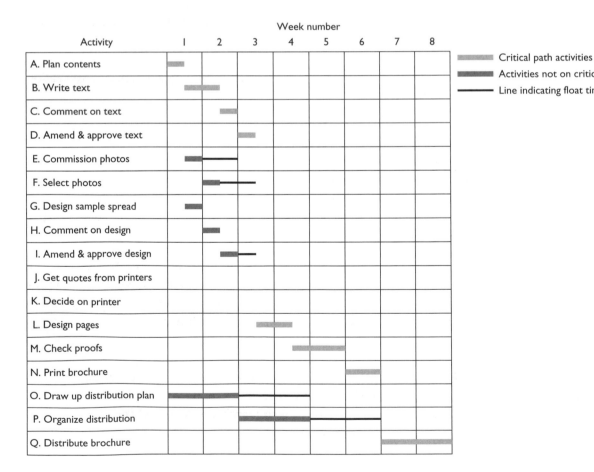

5 Answers to self-assessment questions

Self-assessment 1 on pages 24

1 PESTLE stands for :

   c Political, Economic, Social, Technological, Legal and Environmental

2 a Pressures created by financial institutions, as well as governments and world events, contribute to **economic** factors.
   b **Social** factors may be long term or fleeting. Among the long-term factors are changes in the composition of the population.
   c The policies pursued by government help to shape **political** factors.
   d Consumer protection laws are among the **legal** factors.
   e Among **environmental** factors is the issue of finite resources.
   f Numerous inventions that have changed the way people work are among the **technological** factors.

3 Among an organization's **strengths** are the things it does well and the skills of its staff. Among an organization's **weaknesses** are the gaps in staff skills. **Threats** are those things in the environment that an organization must overcome. **Opportunities** are those things an organization should grasp if it is to develop and prosper.

4 You can keep up-to-date with developments that may affect your organization in the future by:

   ■ reading journals and newspapers;
   ■ talking to suppliers' representatives;
   ■ reading company newsletters and bulletins;
   ■ attending management briefings;
   ■ going on relevant courses;
   ■ talking to colleagues in other parts of the organization, and in other organizations.

5 The most correct statement is (b). Although concern about the environment imposes a variety of legal obligations on organizations, it also presents organizations with new ways of developing. They can, for example, make products with recyclable ingredients, or produce organic foods.

Self-assessment 2 on pages 62

1 At the heart of continuous improvement is the idea that if customers' constantly changing **NEEDS** and wants are to be met, improvements must be made to **PROCESSES** – and consequently products and services – in small **STEPS**, at all levels, forever.

2 You and your staff may have ideas for improvements regarding the physical **CONDITIONS** in which you work, the **RESOURCES** you work with, your relationships with other people within and outside the organization, and the **PROCEDURES** you and your staff follow.

3 A useful tool for mapping out the steps in a process is a **FLOWCHART**.

4 A useful tool for mapping out all the inputs to a process is a **FISHBONE DIAGRAM**.

5 'Five Whys' is a useful technique for getting to the root **CAUSE** of a particular outcome or effect.

6 The 5 Ss stand for:
b Sort, Set in order, Shine, Standardize and Sustain.

7 a The statement that 'Sorting is about finding a place for everything' is FALSE. This is actually a definition of 'setting in order'. Sorting is about getting rid of everything that's not needed.
b The statement that 'Setting in order is about arranging everything in neat piles' is FALSE. 'Setting in order' is actually about finding a place for everything that's needed.
c The statement that 'Standardizing is about establishing standards and setting up systems for such things as storing and handling materials and getting rid of waste' is TRUE.
d The statement that 'Sustaining is all about maintaining standards' is FALSE. Sustaining is more than maintaining standards; it's also about raising standards.

8 If a suggestion scheme is to be successful, you must not only acknowledge suggestions within 24 hours but evaluate them quickly, preferably within one week.

9 In order to maintain commitment among staff to continuous improvement you do not need:
c Appraisal meetings with individual members of staff.

Self-assessment 3 on pages 87–88

1 Systems diagram:

2   The five question words that help you to define a system are:

- WHAT
- WHO
- HOW
- WHEN
- WHERE

3   The four Rs that describe the way that an organization works are:

- RULES
- ROLES
- RESOURCES
- ROUTINES

4   Potential costs and potential benefits could include:

Potential costs
- new capital (buildings, machines and equipment, software and vehicles)
- people (recruiting new people, making people redundant and training people)
- lost output
- higher waste or reject rates
- reduced efficiency

Potential benefits
- reduced operating costs
- improved efficiency
- better motivated staff
- reduction in staff turnover
- increased quality

5   A **GANTT CHART** is in the form of a bar chart which shows all the key activities and when they should begin or end.

6   A **LOGIC DIAGRAM** helps you to identify the key stages in a project and the order in which they should occur.

7   A **CRITICAL PATH DIAGRAM** shows the relationship between different activities, identifying which activities may run in parallel to each other and which must follow on consecutively from each other.

8   a   It is NOT CORRECT that an activity is said to have 'float' if its completion date could be earlier than that shown in the chart. An activity is said to have float if its completion date could be later.
    b   It is CORRECT that float is shown on the chart by the addition of a line. The line extends to the latest possible completion date.
    c   It is NOT CORRECT that an activity is said to have 'slack' if its completion date could be later than that shown in the chart. A statement has slack if it could begin earlier.
    d   It is NOT CORRECT that slack is shown on the chart by the addition of a line. It is float that is shown by a line.

6 Answers to the quick quiz

Answer 1 The six kinds of forces for change represented by the initials PESTLE are political, economic, social, technological, legal and environmental.

Answer 2 Among the environmental forces for change that have affected organizations in the last 30 years or so are the problems presented by pollution and finite resources. Among the effects of industrial pollution have been the depletion of the ozone layer and global warming, which in turn have led to laws banning the use of CFCs and imposing cuts in carbon dioxide emissions. Partly related to concerns over pollution is pressure, some of it legal, to increase the amount of recycling. The growing interest in organic food is also related to environmental concerns.

Answer 3 The initials SWOT stand for strengths, weaknesses, opportunities and threats.

Answer 4 In the cycle of continuous improvement, the next two steps after reviewing what has been done are learning from this review and planning improvements on the basis of what you have learned.

Answer 5 The Japanese name for continuous improvement is kaizen.

Answer 6 The two categories, in addition to physical conditions and resources, into which most small improvements in the workplace fall are relationships and procedures.

Answer 7 The Five Whys technique consists of asking the question 'Why?' five times in relation to a particular process, outcome or event until you get to the root cause of whatever it is you are investigating.

Answer 8 Flowcharting is a useful tool in identifying areas for improvement in a process because it shows the ideal process very graphically and the stages at which it can often go wrong.

Answer 9 In a cause and effect, or fishbone, diagram, the horizontal arrow usually represents a process or problem.

Answer 10 In addition to method and environment, the inputs in a cause and effect diagram may be personnel, equipment, materials, and information.

Answer 11 The other two 5 Ss are Standardize and Sustain.

Answer 12   Red tagging is used in factory 5S programmes as a way of alerting people to a problem. It entails tying red tags to items that have been left lying around, or are dirty, defective or missing.

Answer 13   Once standards for a service or product have been achieved, the next step in the cycle of continuous improvement is to set higher standards. Thus the process of improving a service or product never ends.

Answer 14   A critical path diagram shows how the key project activities link to each other, highlighting the chain of activities – the critical path – which determines when the project begins and ends. A Gantt chart shows all the key activities and when they should begin or end. It doesn't, however, show the relationship between different activities as clearly as a critical path diagram.

7 Certificate

Completion of the certificate by an authorized person shows that you have worked through all the parts of this workbook and satisfactorily completed the assessments. The certificate provides a record of what you have done that may be used for exemptions or as evidence of prior learning against other nationally certificated qualifications.

superseries

Planning Change in the Workplace

....

has satisfactorily completed this workbook

Name of signatory ....

Position ....

Signature ....

Date ....

Official stamp

Pergamon
Flexible
Learning

Fifth Edition

superseries

FIFTH EDITION

Workbooks in the series:

For prices and availability please telephone our order helpline
or email

+44 (0) 1865 474010
directorders@elsevier.com